THE BEDFORD SERIES IN HISTORY AND CULTURE

O9-ABE-414

Other People's Money and How the Bankers Use It

by Louis D. Brandeis

Edited with an Introduction by

Melvin I. Urofsky

Virginia Commonwealth University

BEDFORD BOOKS *of* ST. MARTIN'S PRESS

Boston • New York

For David W. Levy and Philippa Strum
Who share the passion

For Bedford Books
President and Publisher: Charles H. Christensen
General Manager and Associate Publisher: Joan E. Feinberg
History Editor: Niels Aaboe
Editorial Assistant: Richard Keaveny
Managing Editor: Elizabeth M. Schaaf
Production Editor: John Amburg
Copyeditor: Barbara G. Flanagan
Indexer: Steve Csipke
Text Design: Claire Seng-Niemoeller
Cover Design: Richard Emery Design
Cover Art: Morgan Guaranty Trust Company (LC-D4-18602). Courtesy of Library of Congress.

Library of Congress Catalog Card Number: 94 – 65212
Copyright © 1995 by Bedford Books *of* St. Martin's Press

Manufactured in the United States of America.

9 8 7 6 5

f e d c b a

For information, write: St. Martin's Press, Inc., 175 Fifth Avenue, New York, NY 10010
Editorial Offices: Bedford Books *of* St. Martin's Press, 75 Arlington Street, Boston, MA 02116

ISBN: 0 – 312 – 10314 – X (paperback)
ISBN: 0 – 312 – 12257 – 8 (hardcover)

Photo Credits

Page viii: Louis Dembitz Brandeis, 1856 – 1941. LC-USZ62-10583, Library of Congress.
Page 4: Woodrow Wilson. LC-USZ62-21698, Library of Congress.
Page 20: J. P. Morgan. LC-USZ62-8569, Library of Congress.
Page 21: Morgan Guaranty Trust Company. Courtesy of the New York Historical Society, N.Y.C.

Foreword

The Bedford Series in History and Culture is designed so that readers can study the past as historians do.

The historian's first task is finding the evidence. Documents, letters, memoirs, interviews, pictures, movies, novels, or poems can provide facts and clues. Then the historian questions and compares the sources. There is more to do than in a courtroom, for hearsay evidence is welcome, and the historian is usually looking for answers beyond act and motive. Different views of an event may be as important as a single verdict. How a story is told may yield as much information as what it says.

Along the way the historian seeks help from other historians and perhaps from specialists in other disciplines. Finally, it is time to write, to decide on an interpretation and how to arrange the evidence for readers.

Each book in this series contains an important historical document or group of documents, each document a witness from the past and open to interpretation in different ways. The documents are combined with some element of historical narrative—an introduction or a biographical essay, for example—that provides students with an analysis of the primary source material and important background information about the world in which it was produced.

Each book in the series focuses on a specific topic within a specific historical period. Each provides a basis for lively thought and discussion about several aspects of the topic and the historian's role. Each is short enough (and inexpensive enough) to be a reasonable one-week assignment in a college course. Whether as classroom or personal reading, each book in the series provides firsthand experience of the challenge—and fun—of discovering, recreating, and interpreting the past.

Natalie Zemon Davis
Ernest R. May

Preface

Louis D. Brandeis's *Other People's Money and How the Bankers Use It* is a key document of the Progressive era. In few other works do we get the sense of moral outrage and political anger at what the industrialization of the United States had done to traditional social and political values. Brandeis, however, was not a latter-day Don Quixote tilting at imaginary windmills. The industrial revolution of the late nineteenth century had transformed the United States; whatever one might argue about the material benefits factories and mills had brought, one could not deny that "progress" had come at high costs. The price of progress, and what meeting it meant to the United States, is at the heart of both this work and the Progressive movement itself.

This volume, like the others in this series, is designed for use in the classroom. Many of the arguments may strike students as arcane, perhaps even naive, but these arguments can serve to instruct about the mindset of the Progressives, particularly supporters of the Wilsonian New Freedom. Today we take multinational corporations for granted and read about bank profits in terms of billions of dollars per annum. Even the largest of the banks in Brandeis's day would seem relatively small compared to the gigantic bank holding companies of today. Yet in some ways the influence of the banking houses, despite New Freedom and New Deal reforms, remains great; the mergers and leveraged buy-outs of the 1980s would have been impossible without the financial assistance of those large banks able to float multibillion-dollar loans.

The key to understanding *Other People's Money* is not to focus on the financial dealings that Brandeis detailed, but on the moral and social consequences that alarmed him. Although he may have been wrong about the economic aspects of big business, his concerns about what industrial gigantism would do to the nation are still relevant to many people. He may have written in the guise of an economist, but he was really a moralist, and it is that moral aspect of his work that needs emphasis.

The Introduction attempts to place *Other People's Money* in the broader context of the Progressive era, and to locate it in the particular set of political and social concerns that played such a large role in the reform mentality of the time. But the truly enduring value of *Other People's Money* lies in what Brandeis says about American democracy, and in the fact that the worries he had in 1913 still concern many Americans today.

ACKNOWLEDGMENTS

Publishing is a complex process; even in what would appear to be the relatively simple task of reprinting a classic work, many people are involved and many debts undertaken. Charles H. Christensen, president and publisher, Ernest R. May, the series editor, and Sabra Scribner, then the history editor at Bedford, recognized the value of *Other People's Money* and invited me to prepare this edition. David W. Levy and Philippa Strum have, as they have always done, provided insightful comments and useful suggestions regarding the Introduction. Alan Schaffer, Valerie Jean Connor, and Alex Keyssar also read an early draft of the Introduction, and their comments on how to make it more useful to students were greatly appreciated. Niels Aaboe, the current history editor, guided me through the labyrinthine process of preparing the manuscript for publication and making it useful for teachers and students alike. In addition, I am grateful to editorial assistant Richard Keaveny; managing editor Elizabeth Schaaf; production editor John Amburg; and copyeditor Barbara Flanagan.

David W. Levy and Philippa Strum have contributed enormously to the field of Brandeis scholarship, and both have made useful comments on this introduction. Beyond that, they are both good friends whose generosity with colleagues is legendary. The dedication is a token of gratitude and of friendship.

Melvin I. Urofsky

Contents

Figure 1
Louis D. Brandeis, photographed in 1910.

PART ONE

Louis D. Brandeis, Progressivism, and the Money Trust

In August 1912, Boston attorney Louis D. Brandeis journeyed down to Sea Girt, New Jersey, to meet Woodrow Wilson, the governor of New Jersey and the Democratic nominee for president. Wilson's campaign had been foundering for lack of a clearly defined program on how to meet what most Americans considered the key issue of the election, the problem of big business and monopoly. Brandeis had earned a reputation among Progressive reformers for his clear-cut views on monopolies and his proposals on how to end the abuses of large corporations. The issue of how to control big business would be central to the presidential campaign of that year, a campaign that became one of the defining moments of the Progressive era, a period marked by an amazing burst of reform energy directed at the excesses of the great industrial growth that followed the Civil War. After the election, Brandeis explained his ideas about the control of business in a series of magazines articles, which were then published as *Other People's Money;* these essays are key documents in understanding what Progressive reformers feared in the new industrial order and the remedies they proposed.

INDUSTRIALIZATION AND THE REFORM RESPONSE

Progressive reform can best be described as a response to industrialization, which in the years between the Civil War and World War I constituted the most important development in the United States.[1] The transformation of the economy from one dominated by agriculture to one marked by large factories and huge corporations had made the United States one of the leading industrial nations in the world. The American people enjoyed a high standard of living, and immigrants flocked across the ocean in search of economic opportunity and political freedom.

Statistics provide some sense of the enormous economic growth. Between 1870 and 1900, the output of manufactured goods quadrupled. In particular industries the figures are even more spectacular. Between 1870 and 1890, the output of pig iron grew sixfold, that of paper tripled, and the annual sales of manufactured shoes went from $15 million to $250 million. The size of the companies making these products also increased phenomenally, and in 1901 the nation saw its first billion-dollar conglomerate, the U.S. Steel Corporation, which employed 532,000 workers and had an annual payroll of $285 million. Industry was dispersed all over the country; there were centers, of course, but one could find manufacturing concerns from Maine to California, Minnesota to Texas.

While industrialization brought many benefits, it also had high costs. The workers who toiled in factories and mills worked long hours at low wages and often in dangerous conditions. The Chicago department store magnate Marshall Field made over $20,000 a week; he paid his clerks $12 or less for a fifty-nine-hour week. The owners of the great corporations built sumptuous mansions, while their employees lived in tenements so dank and dark they could not even be photographed until the invention of the powder flash in 1887. Mark Twain lambasted the excesses and depradations of the new plutocracy in *The Gilded Age* (1873), and many historians have taken up this theme, pointing out the corruption of the political system, the exploitation of natural resources, the maldistribution of wealth.

By the 1890s many Americans believed that rapid industrialization had caused profound changes and severe problems and that strong measures would have to be taken to curb the glaring injustices created by the new economic order. Progressive reformers proposed a variety of programs to address what they saw as the political, social, and economic inequities that industrialization had spawned.

There is no one program that sums up the Progressive impulse, because the reformers often disagreed among themselves on what should be done. Some advocated measures designed to limit the corrupting effect of big business on the political system; others called for specific laws to protect workers in factories and mines; a group that today we would label as "environmentalists" wanted to protect the nation's natural resources against further exploitation; and some groups emphasized moral and religious teachings.

Not only did the reformers disagree on what should be done, but one cannot always draw a sharp line between reformers and their opponents. People who might agree on creating national parks might disagree on the question of whether women should be able to vote; those who advocated direct election of senators might part company on wages and hours legislation. Many business leaders supported particular reforms, and even the machine bosses, often the target of good-government reformers, frequently joined in support of measures promoting the welfare of urban workers.[2] Some historians have suggested that the word *progressive* came to mean so many different things to so many different groups that it ceased to mean anything at all.[3]

Whatever their disagreements about particulars, and we can examine some of those disagreements in regard to monopoly and the money trust, Progressive reformers did share certain assumptions. They held an optimistic view of the future and believed in progress. They also agreed that society could be improved through deliberate efforts, that they could both enjoy the prosperity that industrialization provided and also cure the evils it had spawned. But to secure a better society, some checks would have to be placed on business. Who would determine these limits, and how would they be enforced? How could orderly growth of the economy be sustained while imposing rigorous restraints on the abuses? These questions formed the core issues of the 1912 presidential campaign.

The incumbent, President William Howard Taft, ran as the conservative candidate, although his four years in the White House had witnessed a fair amount of reform activity. The two leading candidates, the Democrat Woodrow Wilson and the independent Progressive Party nominee, former president Theodore Roosevelt, laid out two seemingly opposite paths they believed the United States should follow.

Roosevelt's program, which he termed the "New Nationalism," called for a recognition that the industrial growth of the late nineteenth century had forever transformed American society. The country would never again be primarily agrarian, with the vast majority of its people living on farms or in small towns. The United States had become, and would remain, an industrial giant, its people residing mainly in large cities and its economic

Figure 2
President Woodrow Wilson, whose New Freedom program relied heavily on the
Brandeis view of the economy and of big business.

life dominated by huge corporations. These companies, Roosevelt declared, had made America great and had given its people the highest
standard of living in the world. They could not be destroyed, but their
power had to be controlled and the interests of the common people
protected.

Social justice, Roosevelt argued, could be secured only through the vigorous efforts of a strong federal government, headed by a vigorous president who would act as a "steward of the public welfare." While he strongly believed in the rights of property, the time had come, he declared, when those who owned property and thought only in terms of personal profit "must now give way to the advocate of human welfare, who rightly maintains that every man holds his property subject to the general right of the community to regulate its use to whatever degree the public welfare may require." He proposed strict regulation of corporations through powerful federal agencies. Roosevelt also embraced a number of ideas put forward by the social justice reformers, including graduated income and inheritance taxes, workers' compensation for industrial accidents, and regulation of labor for women and children.[4]

For Wilson, whose own program to deal with the trusts* would be called the "New Freedom," Roosevelt's solution of big government seemed as bad as or worse than the evil it supposedly addressed, because he feared powerful government as subversive of individual freedom. But while he denounced big business, Wilson originally had no alternative to propose, and when Brandeis offered to meet with him late in August 1912, Wilson eagerly accepted. Louis Brandeis not only had a reputation as an effective reformer, but, more important, he had thought long and hard about the problems of big business and monopoly.

THE BRANDEIS PHILOSOPHY

By the time Brandeis met Wilson in 1912, he had already secured his reputation as one of the leading reformers of the Progressive movement.[5] Born in Louisville in 1856, he had been educated at the Harvard Law School, and in the law he found his great and abiding love. "Law seems so interesting to me in all its aspects," he once told his sister, "it is difficult for me to understand that any of the initiated should not burn with enthusiasm."[6] He and Samuel Warren built up a highly successful law

---

* A *trust* is an organizational device through which a number of firms combine. In practice, shareholders in the individual firms turn in their stock and receive trust certificates. The affairs of all the companies are then run by trustees. *Monopoly* is an economic term describing the market control that a company has. A monopoly is a firm or group of allied companies that effectively controls a market. A trust may or may not be a monopoly, but in the Progressive era reformers used the two terms interchangeably, and when they spoke about trusts, they really meant companies or consolidations that attempted to monopolize their respective markets.

practice in Boston, one that Brandeis headed after Warren left to take over the family paper business.

Brandeis's success resulted in part from his brilliant analytical mind, but also from the new manner in which he practiced law. Prior to the Civil War, clients tended to consult lawyers after whatever had happened that led them either to sue or to be sued. But with the rise of complex markets as well as government regulation in the late nineteenth century, it became too expensive for business to continue in that manner. Now it could be too costly to call a lawyer at the last minute, too wearing to fight a battle that would be taxing even if won. More and more lawyers found themselves asked to advise clients about contemplated future actions, about what to do to avoid going to court. "A lawyer's chief business," said the prominent New York attorney Elihu Root, "is to keep his client out of litigation."[7]

This shift from advocate to counsel imposed new obligations on lawyers. It had been one thing to enter a case with all of the facts available and then to select those most helpful to a client's case. Now attorneys would have to predict future events. New modes of business operation required the lawyer to pay close attention to economic trends and to evaluate developments in which he had not been trained. Creation of trusts and estates and corporate organizations called for planning and analysis of many variables; such planning often involved questions of economics, sociology, psychology, and labor as well as business. The lawyer of the future, Supreme Court Justice Oliver Wendell Holmes, Jr., predicted, would not be the lawbook scholar but "the man of statistics and the master of economics."[8]

No one fit this description better than Louis Brandeis. Eye difficulties in law school had led him to develop his memory, and he could recall nearly all the relevant facts of a case and marshal them with a moment's thought. Later, after his eyes had improved, his wide reading frequently made him more knowledgeable on a subject than so-called expert witnesses. Time and again he would confound his opponents by knowing more about their business than they did. Clients flocked to his office for both his legal abilities and his business advice.[9]

But Brandeis proved to be a lawyer with a difference. Much as he enjoyed the practice of law, his measures of success went far beyond winning cases and making money. As early as the 1890s he began to devote a portion of his time to public service work, an activity unknown to most lawyers of his day. Those successful attorneys who did take time out for "good works" usually engaged in professionally acceptable ventures related to technical reforms of the law, such as the Commission on Uniform State Laws, which attempted to persuade the states to adopt model laws in areas of common interest, such as commercial documents. The idea of serving the public directly, however, struck most lawyers as a strange and ludicrous idea. When the city of Philadelphia fought a corrupt gas company, it could not even hire a local attorney to handle the case and had to go to New York to secure legal representation.[10]

Brandeis started out remitting his fees for public service work and then decided not to accept any payment at all. His friend and client, the Boston department store owner Edward A. Filene, reported a conversation in which Brandeis told him "that he never made a charge for public service . . . that it was his duty as it was mine to help protect the public rights." When Filene argued that Brandeis had an obligation to his family, the latter replied that "he had resolved early in life to give at least one hour a day to public service, and later on he hoped to give fully half his time."[11]

This unusual practice aroused a great deal of comment, and Brandeis responded to it in one interview.

Some men buy diamonds and rare works of art, others delight in automobiles and yachts. My luxury is to invest my surplus effort, beyond that required for the proper support of my family, to the pleasure of taking up a problem and solving, or helping to solve, it for the people without receiving compensation. Your yachtsman or automobilist would lose much of his enjoyment if he were obliged to do for pay what he is doing for the love of the thing itself. So I should lose much of my satisfaction if I were paid in connection with public services of this kind. I have only one life, and it is short enough. Why waste it on things I don't want most? I don't want money or property most. I want to be free.[12]

Thanks in part to his success at the bar,[13] Brandeis began devoting more and more of his time to public service, utilizing not only his legal talents but an astute political sense as well. Like many reformers of his time, Brandeis believed that democracy depended on popular involvement and that the highest calling of an individual was that of a citizen.[14] To this end, at the turn of the century he developed the first "citizens lobby" in Boston, the Public Franchise League, to combat corrupt municipal transit companies. The league is a good example of the different groups who could be found in particular reforms. Primarily middle-class business and professional men, league members also included good-government advocates who opposed municipal corruption for moral as well as political reasons.

Brandeis expanded the idea of public interest advocacy, and in his battle to establish savings bank life insurance in Massachusetts[15] he created a citizens lobby that ranged across the entire social and economic spectrum. While the "interests"—in this case the giant insurance companies—had large amounts of money at their disposal to influence legislators, Brandeis realized that elected officials remained keenly aware of what their constituents wanted, since without voter support legislators would not remain long in their positions. In all the various reforms in which he engaged, Brandeis skillfully orchestrated his supporters to flood newspapers with letters to the editors endorsing the cause, and even more letters and telegrams descended on the State House to impress legislators with how strongly their constituents supported these reforms.

Like many Progressives, Brandeis began his reform work at the local level, fighting corruption in local transportation franchises. But as his horizons broadened, he realized that some problems extended beyond the city limits, and he became involved with statewide matters, such as savings bank insurance.

Throughout his career Brandeis remained firmly committed to a very pragmatic approach to reform. Just as in law one had to know all the facts surrounding a case, so too in politics one had to master the issues. For Brandeis, this meant two things: thoroughly researching a problem in order to understand it completely and then being able to propose a workable solution. Once a group of college students came to see him, eager to help in his reform work. By that time Brandeis had moved onto the national stage, and the students no doubt had visions of working alongside senators and congressmen. Instead, Brandeis told them to start attending sessions of the Boston City Council. There each one of them should take a particular subject—be it zoning, water, or transit—and become totally familiar with all the facts about that issue so that they would know it as well as or better than the council members did. Then, armed with that knowledge, these young reformers would be able to speak authoritatively about their topics, and their views would be heard by the local government. This pragmatic approach proved too prosaic for the starry-eyed students, who left disappointed with Brandeis's suggestion.[16]

Brandeis also recognized that one had to do more than merely identify a problem and then complain about it. One had to offer a workable solution and then rally support behind it. Instead of lamenting rising gas prices, Brandeis proposed a sliding scale system that rewarded both the gas company with higher dividends and the public with cheaper rates. Instead of just attacking the insurance companies for their abuse of workers' policies, Brandeis devised the savings bank insurance plan, by which workers could purchase inexpensive term policies through payments at their local savings bank.

Brandeis's most famous and innovative use of the law for purposes of social reform came in the case of *Muller v. Oregon* (1908).[17] The Oregon legislature, appalled at the fact that women workers in factories often had to work fourteen hours a day or longer, had in 1903 established a maximum ten-hour workday for women. The Oregon statute typified many such reform efforts in the area of protective legislation, laws designed to ameliorate the worst aspects of factory life by imposing safety standards and limiting the number of hours of work. For the most part, such measures normally received judicial approval, since the courts recognized them as legitimate means to protect workers' health and safety.[18] But in the 1905 case of *Lochner v. New York,* the Supreme Court by a narrow 5–4 margin struck down a New York law setting maximum hours for bakery workers. Justice Rufus Peckham denounced the law as unconstitutional because it had no relation to health or safety and therefore exceeded the state's police powers.[19]

Following this decision, Joe Haselbock, the overseer of Curt Muller's Grand Laundry in Portland, Oregon, broke the Oregon law by requiring a Mrs. Elmer Gotcher to work more than ten hours. Muller was charged with violating the ten-hour law, found guilty, and fined ten dollars. After the Oregon Supreme Court upheld the conviction, Muller appealed to the United States Supreme Court, confident that the decision in *Lochner* meant that the Court would find the Oregon law unconstitutional. The National Consumer League, which had been instrumental in securing passage of the ten-hour law, then approached Brandeis to defend the statute. Brandeis agreed to do so, but on three conditions: he would accept no fee for the case; he would have full control over the litigation; and the league would provide him with massive amounts of data on the effects of long working hours on women.

Many reformers considered the *Lochner* decision an insuperable barrier to further protective legislation, but Brandeis saw a way through. One had to show that such a law did, in fact, touch upon worker health and safety, to draw the connection between the law and the conditions of life that had invoked it. "A judge is presumed to know the elements of law," Brandeis had written years earlier, "but there is no presumption that he knows the facts."[20] Brandeis now proceeded to instruct the Court in the facts. After a scant two pages of legal citation, the Brandeis brief set out over a hundred pages of labor statistics and social surveys showing the world's experience in relation to excessive working hours for women.[21] Years later he commented that the brief might properly have been titled "What Any Fool Knows!"

Brandeis's unique approach succeeded, and a unanimous Supreme Court upheld the Oregon law. Justice David Brewer even took the unusual step of mentioning Brandeis by name and pointing to the mass of data he had presented, data that clearly proved that a "woman's physical structure, and the functions she performs in consequence thereof, justify special legislation."[22] The Brandeis brief in *Muller* in many ways changed the practice of law as it related to defending or attacking public policy. Lawyers could no longer evade the responsibility of instructing and advising the courts about the relevant facts. After *Muller*, the production of facts became a prime responsibility of counsel.

With *Muller* Brandeis emerged as a major figure on the national reform stage, his advice sought by Jane Addams (the founder of the Chicago social settlement Hull House), Robert La Follette (the fiery reformer from Wisconsin), Theodore Roosevelt, and others. He became a champion of "scientific management," the theory propounded by Frederick W. Taylor and others that claimed that the labor performed in modern businesses could be analyzed and then redesigned to maximize efficiency.[23] So-called efficiency engineers went into a plant and determined how each task could be done most efficiently and the maximum amount of time that should be allowed for the job, and then trained workers so they could complete their tasks on schedule.

Brandeis saw scientific management as a way not only of increasing productivity but of giving workers greater leisure time and an increased share of the profits. He liked to use the examples of the Tabor Manufacturing Company, which after adopting scientific management reduced prices to its customers by 10 to 15 percent and raised wages by 25 to 30 percent, and the Brighton Mills, which had reduced costs while increasing wages by 45 to 75 percent.[24]

The infatuation with scientific management was one of the few instances in his career when Brandeis confused reality with theory. Organized labor opposed scientific management, and union leaders denounced it as a "speed-up" device to get employees to work faster and harder for little more money, and in most instances that proved to be the case. Brandeis assumed that labor and management would meet together and reason out the benefits of scientific management, and that by cooperating in making it a success, they would share in the savings—greater profits to management and higher wages to labor. In reality, management, with very few exceptions, refused to pass on to workers the savings it achieved. As Brandeis biographer Philippa Strum concluded, Brandeis's "romance with scientific management constituted one of the few times he ignored the advice he gave to others: 'The logic of words should yield to the logic of realities.' "[25]

Brandeis did realize one important thing from his study of scientific management: that many large corporations were managed inefficiently. In part he attributed inefficiency to the very size of the firms and believed that once business grew beyond a certain size it would become inefficient.

But many inefficiencies could be attributed to sheer waste or poor management, and he captured national headlines in late 1910 when he charged that the railroads could save one million dollars a day in operating costs if they adopted a more scientific approach to their business.

The railroads had filed with the Interstate Commerce Commission for a rate increase, and Brandeis had been hired by a group of shippers to represent them at the ICC hearings in opposition to the increase. The railroads claimed they were not making enough money and thus needed higher rates. In detailed cross-examination, Brandeis not only showed that he knew more about the railroad business than many of its executives but forced the railroad people to admit that they had not attempted to achieve greater efficiency in their operations. The ICC turned down the rate request. The railroads, which had first made fun of Brandeis's ideas as either simplistic or wrong, now began to look more closely at what he and scientific management experts proposed. Eventually, however, under public pressure, they began to adopt methods to increase the efficiency of their operations. With the advent of the First World War, however, the railroads again petitioned for a rate increase, and despite the fact that they could not prove they had made significant changes in their management operations, the ICC in December 1914 awarded them increased rates.[26]

By the time Brandeis took on the railroads, he had already become a familiar figure in Washington, and in early 1910 he found himself at the center of the great "scandal" of the Progressive era, the Pinchot-Ballinger controversy. This complicated affair revolved around the Taft administration's natural resource policy and Secretary of the Interior Richard Achilles Ballinger. Under Theodore Roosevelt, millions of acres of public land had been put aside in national parks, national forests, and other preserves. Much of this land contained valuable timber and mineral supplies, and the federal government and private industry had been sparring over what policy would govern private exploitation of the public lands.

Ballinger, a former attorney for northwestern lumber interests, favored a liberal policy regarding timber and mineral mining, but conservationists, headed by Chief Forester Gifford Pinchot, wanted to allow only minimal development. The battle came to a head over the so-called Guggenheim claims, in which a syndicate financed in part by the banker J. P. Morgan was awarded control of coal and timber rights on five thousand acres of land in Alaska. Louis R. Glavis, a land clerk in the Seattle office of the Interior Department that handled Alaskan lands, suspected fraud in the award to the Guggenheims. He communicated with Pinchot, who brought

Glavis's evidence to President Taft. The president asked Ballinger to respond and, upon receipt of Ballinger's reply, exonerated his interior secretary and told him to fire Glavis.

Taft hoped this would be the end of the matter, but instead Pinchot and Glavis took their story to Norman Hapgood, the editor of *Collier's Weekly*, who published the material on November 13, 1909, under the title "The Whitewashing of Ballinger."[27] The public response to the article led to a congressional investigation of the charges, which the Taft administration, with a Republican majority in Congress, hoped to control. To represent *Collier's* interests, Hapgood and publisher Robert Collier asked Brandeis to represent them at the committee hearings, at a fee of $25,000 plus expenses. Pinchot by this time was in open revolt against the administration, so he joined Collier. The committee, composed of six senators and six representatives, was packed with pro-Taft men, but insurgent senator George W. Norris of Nebraska forced congressional leadership to include three men who could be considered independent and open-minded—Senator Edmund H. Madison of Kansas and Representatives Ollie M. James of Kentucky and James Graham of Illinois.

Brandeis wanted to do two things in the hearings: exonerate his clients from any charges of wrongdoing and force a public debate on the nation's land management policies. He, like Pinchot and others, believed that the land should be conserved and that development should be minimal; any exploitation of mineral and timber resources should be closely regulated for the benefit of the public, not for private gain. The Taft administration, of course, was perceived by reformers as closely allied with big business, and Brandeis portrayed its approval of the Guggenheim claims as evidence of its collusion with the trusts.

The conservative members of the committee managed to block any real debate on public policy, but in their efforts to portray Glavis and Pinchot as troublemakers who acted improperly, they set the stage for what proved to be Ballinger's downfall and Taft's embarrassment. Taft had claimed to have read all of the relevant materials provided by Glavis and Pinchot as well as the massive refutation submitted by Ballinger. But something struck Brandeis as wrong, and he concluded that given the volume of the materials and the dates on which Taft supposedly had acted, the president could not have read the materials. Either he had exonerated Ballinger without examining the documents or the presidential letter had been dated earlier than it was actually written. Eventually a clerk in the Interior Department, Frederick Kerby, came forward with evidence that Brandeis's suspicions—which Ballinger and the administration had strenuously denied—were true. Taft had not conducted a thorough investigation, and the letter of exoneration had been prepared by Ballinger's office and backdated. The ensuing uproar caused Ballinger to resign and gave the Taft administration a black eye from which it never recovered. Thus by the time Brandeis joined Woodrow Wilson in the 1912 campaign, he was a national figure widely respected by reformers and feared by big business. But aside from the time he would serve as a close adviser to Wilson, Brandeis still had two major acts to play out in his career, one as the leader of American Zionism during and immediately after World War I, the other as an associate justice of the United States Supreme Court from 1916 to 1939.

Brandeis first became interested in Zionism, the movement to recreate a Jewish homeland in Palestine, around 1910, when he served as a mediator in the great New York garment workers strike of that year.[28] There he had met Jews of a type he had not known before, Eastern European immigrants who quoted the prophets in Yiddish and spoke in terms of social justice and democracy. A while later the journalist Jacob de Haas interviewed Brandeis for a Boston Jewish newspaper and in the conversation introduced Brandeis to the ideas of Theodor Herzl, the founder of the modern Zionist movement.

Brandeis joined the movement but took no active interest until August 1914, when he agreed to head an emergency committee to provide aid for the Jewish settlements in Palestine, whose economic ties to Europe had been cut off by the war. Brandeis quickly energized the American Zionist movement and increased its membership from 12,000 in 1914 to more than 186,000 in 1919. He used his connections with the Wilson administration to facilitate the shipment of relief supplies to Palestine and in 1917 played a key role in securing Wilson's endorsement of the Balfour Declaration, in which the British promised to support a Jewish homeland in Palestine after the war.

Brandeis's achievements as a Zionist leader derived not from his religious views but from his experiences and beliefs as an American Progressive reformer. He applied the organizational and political skills he had learned in reform work to Zionism; he treated it as a problem that required a solution, and he forged one that had a particularly American flavor, in fact one that reflected his own Jeffersonian belief in democracy, economic cooperation, and social justice. He also overcame the fears of many American Jews that support of the Zionists would somehow undermine their own status as Americans.[29] In doing so he transformed Zionism from a primarily religious movement to one that was more political and practical, and it was that practicality that in large measure accounted for its later success in helping to establish the state of Israel.

Wilson, after his election, wanted to name Brandeis attorney general, but the outcry from the business community forced him to back down. Nonetheless he used the Boston attorney as an informal but highly influential adviser and in 1916 nominated him to the Supreme Court. Following a bruising four-month confirmation fight, marked by an aggressive smear campaign waged by business as well as some anti-Semitism,[30] Brandeis was confirmed and took his seat in June 1916.

During his twenty-three years on the bench, Brandeis carved out a lasting reputation not only as one of the most skilled legal craftsmen to sit on the Court but also as one of its greatest jurists. His carefully written opinions became models of how the Court should explain its decisions, and, especially in dissent, Brandeis carried through on his earlier demand that there be more life in the law, that Court decisions reflect the facts of the real world and not the sterile logic of words.

Brandeis had such an important impact on the Court because during his tenure the judicial agenda was changing. Until 1940, much of the Court's work had to do with economic measures as legislatures attempted to regulate business and labor. Conservatives dominated the Court during this time and blocked some of these regulatory statutes; during the 1930s, large parts of Franklin Roosevelt's New Deal were struck down as unconstitutional. But the agenda was changing, and Brandeis did much to lay the foundation for that change. He argued that the courts should not be in the business of second-guessing the legislatures on economic policy and that unless a clear-cut constitutional prohibition existed, legislatures ought to be free to pursue what they considered appropriate policy.[31]

At the same time, the Court was hearing more and more cases regarding civil liberties and civil rights, and here Brandeis, joined by Justices Oliver Wendell Holmes, Jr., and Harlan Fiske Stone, laid the foundation for the great explosion in judicially protected individual rights after World War II. It was Brandeis who first suggested that the Fourteenth Amendment's due process clause might also apply the Bill of Rights to the states, the idea that became known as "incorporation."[32] And perhaps most important, Brandeis established the basis for the modern jurisprudence of free speech. He first joined with Holmes in the World War I espionage cases, in which Holmes set out the notion of a "clear and present danger" test* as a guide by which government could regulate expression.[33] But within a short time both men changed their minds and decided that even in wartime, free

---

*The clear and present danger test allowed government to restrict speech and newspaper publication if it could show that the content of the speech presented an immediate and obvious danger to public safety or national security.

expression had to be protected. Not until 1927, however, did Brandeis enunciate a compelling reason why speech had to be protected, and he based it on his belief in the importance of citizen participation in the political process. People had to be free to speak their minds without fear, he argued, so that society could benefit from all points of view and men and women would be able to engage fully in the debate that is at the heart of the democratic process.[34]

By the time he retired from the Court in 1939, Brandeis had become practically an American icon. Both conservatives and liberals praised his record on the Court, and even today his opinions continue to be cited by both conservative and liberal justices. His life, which has been celebrated in a number of works, is in some ways heroic: the man set out to confront and overcome great challenges, and in his various endeavors he appears to have done so. He was not, however, a saint, although there is a tendency to treat his life as free of all blemishes. He could be a difficult person and often set standards that were difficult for others to follow. He was a ruthless foe and not always a gracious winner, once telling someone he had bested not to be a "cry baby." He saw life as hard and in some ways was as much a Darwinian as the conservatives who believed only in the survival of the fittest; the difference is that he wanted to place some limits on the predatory nature of humans and they did not. He did not, however, believe that the state should undertake programs to support those who could not survive in the marketplace—that is, those who could not make a go of it in business.

One area in which he has been faulted is his extensive extrajudicial activities while on the bench. Brandeis had such a confident view of his own integrity that he engaged in activities that, by today's standards, would be improper for a judge. He did not take bribes but rather engaged in political activities, advising both Wilson and Franklin Roosevelt while on the bench and, through Harvard law professor Felix Frankfurter, supporting a variety of other reform programs in the 1920s and 1930s.[35] The activist side of his nature just could not be stilled by the judge's robes.

BRANDEIS, WILSON, AND THE TRUST ISSUE

His Zionist and Court careers were still ahead of him when Brandeis began to advise President Wilson on the problems of the trusts, and by 1912 Brandeis had developed certain ideas about American society and the dangers it faced from industrialization. He was particularly concerned about what he saw as the troublesome relationship between monopoly and finance.

Brandeis had first learned about the interrelation between finance and monopoly when he opposed the efforts of the great finance banker J. P. Morgan to monopolize New England railroads through the merger of the New Haven and other regional lines.[36] In a letter to the journalist Norman Hapgood in 1911 Brandeis wrote:

> The honest financiers who are using, as bankers and insurance company managers, etc., the money of others, realize that they hold the money in trust for its owners and must be fair to the beneficiaries. They do not realize, however, that the power which the control of other people's money gives them to grant or to withdraw credit, is a trust for the public—a power to be exercised impartially as the applicant for credit is entitled to it. They exercise their power regardless of that trust, ignoring the square deal, and it amounts practically to their playing the industrial game with loaded dice. . . . By controlling the money of other people at the same time that they are engaged in industrial and other occupations, they suppress competition and get other advantages by means that are illegal.[37]

Later that year, he told a reporter that "the control of capital is, as to business, what the control of water supply is to life. The economic menace of past ages was the dead hand which gradually acquired a large part of all available lands. The greatest economic menace of today is a very live hand—these few able financiers who are gradually acquiring control over our quick capital."[38] It would be one thing if the bankers used their own money; after all, people had a right to refuse to lend their own capital. But bankers held other people's money and therefore had an obligation to manage it in a fair and equitable manner. This they were not doing, and as a result "the fetters which bind the people are forged from the people's own gold."[39]

The extent to which the country had in fact come under the sway of big business had been detailed by the conservative Wall Street publisher John Moody, who believed that this development boded well for the future prosperity of the country. According to Moody, 318 industrial corporations dominated American manufacturing by the end of 1903. These companies had a total capital of $7.25 billion, controlled more than 5,300 distinct plants, and accounted for 40 percent of the manufacturing capital in the country. Of these firms, 236 had been organized within the previous six years.[40] Moody added transportation and utility companies to industries and concluded that 445 corporations, capitalized at $20.4 billion, represented some 8,664 original companies that had been swallowed up in mergers. (Brandeis would deal with these developments in *Other People's Money*; see chapter II.)

Moody saw these developments as good, as he did the close connections between Wall Street financiers and industry. He identified two major groupings, one headed by banker J. P. Morgan and the other by the founder of Standard Oil, John D. Rockefeller. There were some lesser investment groupings, such as the interests clustered around railroad magnate E. H. Harriman, but in all important matters the Rockefeller and Morgan groups dominated American industry and also controlled some of the leading banking and insurance institutions of the country. Thus the Rockefeller interests laid claim to the National City Bank, Hanover National, United States Trust, and a host of smaller banks as well as the Equitable and Mutual of New York insurance companies, while the Morgan group included First National Bank, Chase National, and the New York Life Insurance Company (See chapter I.)

Moody was confident that such developments were in the best interests of the nation. Moreover, lest any misunderstand his story, he made it clear that "these two great groups of capitalists and financiers are [not] in any real sense rivals or competitors for power, or that such a thing as 'war' exists between them. For, as a matter of fact, they are not only friendly, but they are allied to each other by many close ties. . . . It is felt and recognized on every hand in Wall Street to-day, that they are harmonious in nearly all particulars."[41]

Brandeis and many other reformers found Moody's statistics alarming, and, rather than cheer these developments, they warned of the dire consequences for the nation. They did so on economic grounds but also for social and political reasons. Brandeis believed in a small-unit economy, that is, one of small manufacturers in which every person had the opportunity to succeed. In his mind, a small-unit economy made political democracy possible. The most feasible socioeconomic framework for democracy was one in which the bulk of productive and distributive work was done through small agencies—independent farmers, merchants, and manufacturers. The division of wealth, labor, and responsibility among as many people as possible assured to each not only a voice but also a stake in the growth and stability of society. He yearned, perhaps naively and inaccurately, for the days when "nearly every American boy could look forward to becoming independent as a farmer or mechanic,"[42] not out of nostalgia but out of the belief that such opportunity made democracy possible.

Over and over he emphasized the connection between individual opportunity and political freedom.[43] "You cannot have true American citizenship," he declared in testimony before the Senate, "you cannot preserve political liberty, you cannot secure American standards of living, unless some degree of industrial liberty accompanies it."[44] The greatest danger to the people of the United States, he warned, "is in becoming, as they are gradually more and more, a class of employees."[45] Brandeis, however, was no leveler; he did not want to make everyone "equal." Part of the price of opportunity was that some people would fail, and as he told his daughter Susan, "You will do well to remember that life is hard." The competition of life and of the economy, with both the harshness and the rewards, was always acceptable to him; life itself should not be easy but should be a continuous challenge.

The argument made by people such as Theodore Roosevelt that the growth of large corporations represented a basic and irreversible law of economic development did not impress him, nor did Brandeis accept the claim that the industrial giants operated more efficiently than did small companies and could as a result provide the American people with a higher standard of living. To him, this reasoning missed the entire point of what America meant. He maintained that "it is absolutely essential in order that men develop that they be properly fed and properly housed, and that they have proper opportunities of education and recreation." A free nation demanded no less; but "we may have all these things and have a nation of slaves."[46] Did the United States, as a nation, value material comfort over freedom of opportunity? In the two decades prior to World War I, many reformers saw in the growth of big business a threat that America could lose that freedom.

But how could one preserve these virtues when more and more of the American economy appeared to be falling under the control of gigantic corporations that monopolized industry? Theodore Roosevelt accepted such development as unavoidable and wanted to use the power of government both to regulate the corporations and to punish those who abused their power. The United States, Roosevelt declared, should adopt "the policy of attacking not the mere fact of combination, but the evils and wrongdoing which so frequently accompany combination. . . . We should enter upon a course of supervision, control, and regulation of these great corporations—a regulation which we should not fear, if necessary, to bring to the point of control of monopoly prices."[47] Brandeis firmly opposed the ideas that big business was inevitable and that it should be regulated by big government, and when he met Wilson at Sea Girt, the Boston attorney laid out a plan that in essence became Wilson's New Freedom.

Both men agreed that big government and big business posed threats to the democratic nature of American society. Brandeis proposed that government, instead of regulating business, regulate competition and establish clear rules for how industry could conduct itself in the marketplace. Once such rules had been enacted, Brandeis believed, big business would not be able to compete successfully against smaller, more efficient entrepreneurs, and the problem of monopoly would be solved by the marketplace itself.

In his first speech after meeting with Brandeis, Wilson proved himself an apt pupil. He attacked Roosevelt's proposal to regulate monopoly and asked, "What has created these monopolies? Unregulated competition." Wilson now proposed remedial legislation to "so restrict the wrong use of competition that the right use of competition will destroy monopoly." A few days later he again attacked monopoly as destructive of both economic and political freedom. At Sioux Falls, South Dakota, the Democratic candidate declared that "the alternative to regulating monopoly is to regulate competition."[48] Wilson now wanted more details and asked Brandeis to explain how competition could be regulated and what specific measures should be taken. Brandeis did so and also set out in detail how Wilson and Roosevelt, and their followers, differed in viewing the key problem of economic concentration:

> The two parties differ fundamentally regarding the economic policy which the country should pursue. The Democratic Party insists that competition can and should be maintained in every branch of private industry; that competition can and should be restored in those branches of industry in which it has been suppressed by the trusts; and that, if at any future time monopoly should appear to be desirable in any branch of industry, the monopoly should be a public one — monopoly owned by the people and not by the capitalists. The New Party, on the other hand, insists that private monopoly may be desirable in some branches of industry, or at all events, is inevitable; and that existing trusts should not be dismembered or forcibly dislodged from those branches of industry in which they have already acquired a monopoly, but should be made "good" by regulation. In other words, the New Party declares that private monopoly in industry is not necessarily evil, but may do evil; and that legislation be limited to such laws and regulations as should attempt merely to prevent the doing of evil. The New Party does not fear commercial power, however great, if only methods for regulation ever have been or can be devised to remove the menace inherent in private monopoly and overweening commercial power.[49]

The New Freedom, as Wilson and Brandeis envisioned it, would constitute a limited but effective program consisting of tariff reduction, revision of the Sherman Antitrust Act, and reform of the banking system. The

Figures 3 and 4

Left: J. P. Morgan. Morgan's control of credit gave him the dominant voice in many of the nation's largest industries. *Above:* The "House of Morgan" on Wall Street was the literal and figurative capital of the "money trust."

Sherman Act, passed in 1890, in its basic provisions outlawed "every contract, combination in the form of trust or otherwise, or conspiracy in restraint of trade or commerce." What these words actually meant had not been clear at the time of the act's passage, and in subsequent court cases conservative justices had been reluctant to apply the measure to big business. Wilson and Brandeis believed that a much more specific law was needed which spelled out in detail the type of activities that would be prohibited. Such a law, by creating a truly competitive environment, would preclude the development of future monopolies and whittle down the power of those already created. Banking reform was important because both men believed that at the heart of the larger problem of monopoly stood a money trust; that is, a combination of big banks that controlled the financial resources of the country. Because of the power that banks wielded in an industrialized economy, banking was the most pernicious of all monopolies.

Adding fuel to Wilson's charges, Representative Arsène Pujo of Louisiana, head of the House Banking and Currency Committee, held hearings during the 1912 campaign to discover whether a money trust actually existed and, if it did, the extent of its powers. The committee called leading bankers such as J. P. Morgan to the stand and uncovered a tangled web of connections among the banks, the major industries on whose boards banker representatives sat, and the stock exchange, where the banks placed the securities of those same companies. In his articles based on the committee hearings, Brandeis elaborated on these findings, describing how Morgan's representatives dominated all the different companies involved in an industry, with one company selling raw materials to another, a third distributing products, a fourth handling the financial arrangements, and all working not to promote efficiency and competition but to enhance the power and profits of the Morgan firm (see pp. 171–74). The committee made several recommendations, including stricter enforcement of the antitrust laws and abolishing interlocking directorates. "The Money Trust," charged the *Philadelphia North American*, "is the Wall Street system. But it is clearer to say that the Stock Exchange is the machinery through which the Money Trust operates—in unloading upon the public its manufactured securities[50] and in maintaining its control of prices, of cash, and of credit."[51]

Although Kansas editor William Allen White disdainfully described the ideas of the two men as about as different as Tweedledum and Tweedledee, in fact Wilson and Roosevelt laid out for the American people clear philosophical differences in the 1912 campaign. They offered the electorate a choice between, on the one hand, accepting big business and regulating it through big government and, on the other, attempting to halt further consolidation and re-create an economic environment based on true competition; one candidate would regulate monopoly, the other would destroy it.

In the election, Wilson polled only 41.9 percent of the popular vote but carried forty of the forty-eight states and won a clear majority of 435 ballots in the electoral college. Roosevelt received 27.4 percent of the popular vote and six states, and Taft 23.2 percent and two states. Wilson now had his mandate, and on a bright and sunny morning in March 1913, the new president summoned "all honest men, all patriotic, all forward-looking men, to my side. God helping me, I will not fail them, if they will but counsel and sustain me."[52]

THE NEW FREEDOM
AND BANKING REFORM

Wilson's first item of business centered on meeting one of the key planks of the Democratic Party platform, the lowering of tariff rates on imported goods and raw materials. Ever since the Civil War, business interests and their Republican allies in Congress had pushed tariff rates higher and higher, and the Democrats charged that such rates benefited monopolies and burdened farmers and consumers. Despite bitter opposition from industries unwilling to give up tariff protection, Wilson pushed through the Underwood Tariff of 1913, the first significant cut in tariff rates since the Civil War. He then turned to reform of the banking and currency system.

In the early days of the Republic, the Bank of the United States, created by Alexander Hamilton in 1791, had served effectively as a central bank. Its functions had included holding government deposits, issuing currency, and lending money to smaller banks. This last function was, and is, a key function of a central bank, whether it is a private bank like the Bank of the United States or a government agency like the current Federal Reserve Bank. Small banks do not always have the resources to meet local banking needs, and by serving as a "banker's bank," a central bank can put additional resources into areas where they are needed. Also, because it is a creditor of the local banks, the central bank can impose standards of banking conduct and thus regulate credit.

The Bank of the United States worked well, but President Andrew Jackson denounced it as a monopoly and killed it off in the early 1830s. The country managed without a central bank, but with increasingly severe dislocations in its financial affairs due to the absence of a means to regulate currency supplies. During the Civil War, the enormous need of the North for additional banking and monetary resources led Congress to enact the National Bank Act in 1863 and then amend it the following year. Under the new system, existing state banks as well as new corporations could apply for federal charters and become national banks. To qualify, an institution had to meet certain minimal capital requirements and to invest one-third of that capital in government securities. In return, a national bank would receive U.S. Treasury notes that it could then issue as currency. Moreover, Congress placed a tax on state bank notes,[53] which in effect drove them out of circulation and induced many reluctant state banks to seek federal charters so they could issue federal notes. The new system eliminated much of the chaos and uncertainty in the nation's currency system, but it did not address other issues, such as the ability to control currency in response to shifting demands. In addition, the country still had no central bank to respond to the fiscal strains that industrialization placed on the banking system; no means existed to mobilize the banking reserves of the country, and the totally uncontrolled money supply bore no relation to the needs of business or agriculture. If, for example, the southern and western states needed additional money reserves during harvest seasons, no mechanism existed to shift surplus reserves from other parts of the country.

These deficiencies became evident in the Panic of 1907, which resulted in widespread demand for reform. The boom years following the Depression of 1893 had led American industry to overbuild, and by 1907 neither domestic nor foreign markets could absorb all of the output. Throughout the year, security prices fell, and industrial production took a sharp downturn. As early as March, banks started calling on the federal government for help, and the Treasury deposited more than $70 million in customs receipts in New York banks. By October the situation had grown desperate, and Secretary of the Treasury George B. Cortelyou went to New York to join J. P. Morgan and other bankers in shifting funds from bank to bank to stave off collapse. When the resources of the private banks proved inadequate, Cortelyou threw in additional millions of government funds. In November the government issued an additional $100 million in Treasury certificates and $50 million in Panama Canal bonds and sold them to the banks on credit so the banks could issue additional currency. Whether or not this last measure proved decisive, by January the panic had ended and recovery had begun.[54]

A number of people called the economic crisis a "banker's panic," caused by the overextension of credit and the inadequacy of the system, and Congress named a National Monetary Commission to investigate the banking system and recommend reforms. Nelson W. Aldrich, the conservative senator from Rhode Island who was also John D. Rockefeller's father-in-law, headed the commission, which intensively studied the need for reform of the banking and currency system and made recommendations to Congress in 1911 and 1912. But while nearly everyone agreed on the need for reform, the Aldrich proposal highlighted how far apart different groups stood on the question of what sort of banking system the country should have.

Drawn up primarily by bankers, the Aldrich proposal represented the banking community's views. The plan provided for one central bank, a National Reserve Association, with capital of no less than $100 million and with fifteen branches in different parts of the country. Both the branches and the central bank were to be privately controlled by the local banks on the basis of their capitalization (the amount their stock was worth), thus guaranteeing control to the large banks associated with the Morgan and Rockefeller interests. The National Reserve Association would issue currency, based on gold reserves and commercial paper,[55] and that currency would be the liability of the bank, not of the government. The association would also carry member bank reserves (that is, serve as a depository for smaller country banks), determine discount rates (the rates at which it would lend money to smaller banks), buy and sell securities on the open market, and also serve as the bank for the federal government.[56]

The Democratic Party, which traced its antipathy to central banking back to Jacksonian times, immediately rejected the Aldrich plan, and more radical members of the party denounced it as a resurrection of the old Bank of the United States. William Jennings Bryan, the three-time Democratic presidential candidate and the titular leader of the party, insisted that the federal government, not a central bank, should control the system and issue currency, a proposal that sent shudders up and down Wall Street. Wilson and the moderate wing of the party recognized that some reform of the system was necessary, but at the time of his election he had no specific plan to offer.

In January and February 1913, Representative Carter Glass, head of a subcommittee of the House Banking and Currency Committee, along with H. Parker Willis, the subcommittee's banking expert, held hearings at which a parade of bankers endorsed the basic provisions of the Aldrich scheme. By the time of Wilson's inaugural, it appeared that the new president had adopted their plan and would present it as soon as he had cleared away the problem of the tariff. The Glass-Willis proposal consisted of a centralized, privately controlled reserve system of not more than twenty independent reserve banks. Wilson's one contribution had been "an altruistic Federal Reserve Board in Washington to supervise the system," a "capstone" to the system. The significant difference between the Aldrich and the Glass-Willis plans was the absence of the powerful National Reserve Association in the Glass-Willis scheme; otherwise, both plans were cautious and conservative, designed to win the support of the business and banking communities by leaving control in private hands. While the proposed Glass-Willis plan would have been more flexible than the existing system in meeting the nation's banking needs and would have provided greater credit opportunities for small bankers, it would not have significantly reduced the power of the big Wall Street banks.

Wilson decided to keep the Glass-Willis plan secret, not wanting to divert attention from the fight over tariff reform. But word of the plan leaked out, and when William Jennings Bryan, now Wilson's secretary of state, learned the details, he immediately announced his opposition. Bryan wanted the Federal Reserve Board to be composed solely of government-appointed officials and to have extensive regulatory powers over private banks; he also demanded that issuing currency be solely a government function. Secretary of the Treasury William Gibbs McAdoo then came up with a third plan, in which a central bank would be part of the Treasury Department.[57]

While this scenario played out behind the scenes in Washington, Brandeis had begun work on a series of articles based on the Pujo committee hearings on the money trust, but ranging far beyond what the committee had covered. While Brandeis would play a critical role in resolving the dispute over banking reform, the articles would not be published until the end of 1913 and the beginning of 1914 and would have their greatest impact on the adoption of the administration's antitrust legislation.

As soon as the Pujo committee published its report in March 1913, Brandeis read it and told Samuel Untermyer, the committee's counsel, "It is admirable, and most of your recommendations I should heartily approve. In some respects it seems to me that the recommendations do not go far enough."[58] Brandeis began to gather additional information, writing to people all over the country to garner examples of banker management.[59] (He used these examples in chapter 9.) Brandeis often ran into difficulty in his research, since bankers and businessmen frequently refused to provide him with the information he sought, and he had to get it, when he could, from other sources. Sometimes he could not find the proof he needed for some of his assertions and had to content himself with hinting at the size of the problem.

In the midst of Brandeis's research, he was summoned to Washington by Wilson to help the president decide on the final shape of the banking reform bill. Brandeis distrusted the big banking houses almost to the point of obsession and had once said:

> We have no place in American democracy for the money king, not even for the merchant prince. We are confronted in the twentieth century, as we were in the nineteenth, with an irreconcilable conflict. Our democracy cannot endure half free and half slave. The essence of the trust is a combination of the capitalist, by the capitalist, and for the capitalist.[60]

Brandeis came to the White House on June 11, 1913, and convinced Wilson of the rightness of Bryan's arguments: government alone should issue currency, and government should control the banking system for the good of the country. The American people, he told the president, would not be content to have bankers controlling the system, for their judgments would always be clouded by private interests. To bolster Wilson's resolve, Brandeis sounded a dire warning that "the conflict between the policies of the Administration and the desires of the financiers and of big business, is an irreconcilable one. Concessions to the big business interests must in the end prove futile."[61]

Wilson now moved forward and proposed the Federal Reserve Act, which in its final form provided for government control of the banking system and the issue of currency. Wilson proposed the measure to Congress on June 23, 1913, and signed it into law by the end of the year. It was the most important constructive piece of legislation in his administration and one of the most important in the history of the nation.

The Federal Reserve Act provided for twelve regional banks, owned and controlled by the private banks in each region. The regional Federal Reserve bank would hold a certain percentage of the member banks' assets in reserve, which they would lend as member banks need funds at an interest rate (discount); they would also issue Federal Reserve notes, which would become the country's sole form of paper currency and which would be backed by the government. A Federal Reserve Board, named by the president, would supervise and regulate the system. All national banks had to join the system, and other banks were encouraged to do so. By the late 1920s, more than 80 percent of the nation's banks belonged to the system.

Imperfect in many ways, the Federal Reserve Act struck that careful balance between private control and public supervision that Wilson and Brandeis so idealized. Banking remained in private hands, but bankers now had to observe rules designed to limit their influence and keep their transactions honest. Within a short time the measure won the approval of the banking community, especially the smaller country banks freed from reliance on Wall Street. Senator Robert M. La Follette of Wisconsin denounced it as a "big bankers' bill," a charge echoed by radicals such as Senator Joseph H. Bristow of Kansas and Representative Charles A. Lindbergh of Minnesota. But they, and others, misunderstood the nature of Wilsonian reform.

The New Freedom remained at all times a conservative program, designed not to restructure society but to remove what Wilson, Brandeis, and other reformers saw as artificial impediments to free competition. To the extent that it favored popular democracy against a wealthy elite, it was progressive, but Wilson and Brandeis always opposed using government power as a counterbalance to private power. They wanted minimal government interference in the economy and in life and believed that if they could develop clear rules of regulation, that would be sufficient. In the long run, big government did come, and, ironically enough, it was unleashed by the Wilson administration to meet the challenges of World War I.[62]

OTHER PEOPLE'S MONEY AND ANTITRUST LEGISLATION

Even as Wilson oversaw the final stages of passage and signed the Federal Reserve Act into law, *Harper's Weekly*[63] in November 1913 published "Breaking the Money Trust, Part I: Our Financial Oligarchy," the first of nine articles that Brandeis would assemble (along with one additional article) as *Other People's Money and How the Bankers Use It*.[64] More than any other document of the Progressive era, *Other People's Money* captured the anger that reformers felt about monopoly and their fears about what bigness could do to American democracy.

The response to the articles and book was predictable, with reformers hailing Brandeis's exposé and members of the business and banking community condemning it. One enthusiastic reader told Brandeis that "no man ever did so much to enlighten the people." Senator Robert M. La Follette of Wisconsin called *Other People's Money* "epoch-making," while the *Washington Star* termed it "concrete and amazingly circumstantial, clear and forceful." B. H. Meyer of the Interstate Commerce Commission told Brandeis, "I had never before seen these matters focused so intensively and brought within the range of understanding of the average intelligent citizen." Bankers, understandably, viewed the work far less charitably. Frank A. Vanderlip, president of the National City Bank of New York, called the whole notion of a money trust "moonshine," and denounced the findings of both the Pujo committee and the articles as a "bureau of misinformation." Other businessmen had similar comments.[65]

Although the Pujo committee had originally intended to look at the money trust as a prelude to banking reform, Brandeis had always seen the power of Wall Street financiers as part of a larger problem, that of monopoly and, in many ways, of bigness itself. By the time *Harper's* began publishing the articles on November 8, banking reform had been secured. But the reform affected the internal operations of the banking system and did not address the larger issue of curbing the power of the banks to create and control big business. So in the series Brandeis addressed the monopoly issue as well as the money trust, looking forward to the revision of the Sherman Antitrust Act.

In the various articles Brandeis engaged in what some commentators have called "serious muckraking," exposing the evils of financial capitalism in a responsible manner, using sensational facts not for the sake of sensationalism but to make important points. Muckraking was central to the heart of Progressive reform, since it served an important tenet of the reformers. Brandeis and others believed that for democracy to work, the citizens had to take an active, engaged, and, above all, informed part in government. People could not be expected to solve difficult social problems if they did not understand the issues involved; they could not be expected to act against evils if they did not know that the evils existed. "Publicity is justly recommended as a remedy for social and industrial diseases," Brandeis wrote. "Sunlight is said to be the best of disinfectants; electric light the most efficient policeman."[66] (See chapter V.)

Investigative journalists such as Ida Tarbell, Ray Stannard Baker, Lincoln Steffens, and others thus performed an important public service.[67] They informed the citizenry of problems that demanded action; once armed with that information, the people could act. Perhaps the most striking example of muckraking was *The Jungle* (1906), Upton Sinclair's exposé of the filth and corruption in the Chicago meatpacking yards, which led to the passage of the Meat Inspection Act in 1906. Brandeis hoped that his articles on the money trust would have the same impact and lead to effective antitrust legislation.

In addition to exposing what he considered betrayal of the people's trust, Brandeis informed *Other People's Money* with an important underlying philosophy, namely that excellence and achievement derive from the struggle of life or, in the economic sphere, from competition. Brandeis never questioned the basic rightness of the free enterprise system; that it had its defects he freely admitted, and he did a great deal to formulate proposals on how these should be corrected. His own success, however, imbued him with a sense of the great opportunities awaiting the hard worker; great demands and great effort could lead to great rewards. He had differed with many of his fellow reformers in Boston when he insisted that risk capital deserved greater returns than capital invested in safe ventures, although he condemned outright speculation. Despite his advocacy of such measures as savings bank life insurance or wage and hours regulation, Brandeis cannot be said to have greatly concerned himself with the weak.[68] Those who competed had to bear the losses as well as enjoy the victories; he would back measures that prevented the strong from taking unfair advantage of the weak, but he opposed programs that tried to give a leg up to those on the bottom. He reveled in the competition of life and of the economy, with both the harshness and the rewards, since success and failure contributed to a person's growth; life should be a challenge.

At least one of the thousands of people who read the articles took them seriously. Woodrow Wilson read the series carefully, making notes in the margins[69] and then utilizing them in a special message to Congress in late January 1914. The president initially had been hesitant about pushing forward on antitrust legislation. There had been a slight recession in 1913, and his more conservative advisers urged him to let business adjust to the tariff and banking acts before he proposed more legislation. Secretary of Agriculture David Houston advised the president "to make haste slowly," while the Boston financier Henry Lee Higginson pleaded with Wilson to forgo any new legislation that could affect industry and commerce.[70]

But from Boston also came advice from Louis Brandeis—Be Bold! Antitrust legislation was essential not only to fulfill the New Freedom but also to "politically satisfy the demands of the very large number of progressive Democrats and the near Democrats who are already beginning to express some doubts" regarding the administration's courage. The so-called business depression "cannot be ended or lessened by any course which the administration may take. . . . The fearless course is the wise one."[71]

The president's message to Congress showed how carefully he had read Brandeis's articles, for the proposals he made responded directly to the problems Brandeis illustrated. Wilson called for outlawing interlocking directorates (discussed at length in chapter III); giving the Interstate Commerce Commission power to supervise capital financing and the issuance of securities by the railroads; creating a federal commission to provide businesses with advice and information, but not having regulatory power;[72] establishing penalties for individuals as well as corporations guilty of malpractices; and providing that any facts or judgments decided in government suits would not have to be reproven in private damage suits.[73] On reading the speech, Brandeis commented with satisfaction to his brother that Wilson "has paved the way for about all I have asked for and some of the provisions specifically are what I got into his mind at my first interview."[74] As the Clayton bill, embodying the president's proposal, moved through Congress, Brandeis suggested several ways to strengthen particular provisions and testified on its behalf before the Senate Committee on Interstate Commerce.[75]

But the final version of the Clayton Antitrust Act, passed by Congress on June 5, 1914, disappointed many Progressives. When the bill had first been introduced, according to Senator James Reed of Missouri, "it was a raging lion with a mouth full of teeth. It has degenerated to a tabby cat with soft gums, a plaintive mew, and an anaemic appearance. It is a sort of legislative apology to the trusts, delivered hat in hand, and accompanied by assurances that no discourtesy is intended." Even the president complained that the Senate Judiciary Committee had watered the bill down beyond recognition.[76]

Instead of outright bans on exclusive selling contracts (agreements requiring retailers to sell only one firm's product and not its competitors'), interlocking directorates, or interlocking stockholdings, the prohibitions all had mitigating phrases such as "where the effect may be to substantially lessen competition." Now the government, instead of merely having to prove that an exclusive selling contract existed, would also have to prove that it "substantially lessened competition." The original aim of the act had been to make the government's burden of proof easier by outlawing certain actions completely; for all practical purposes, the antitrust measures of the Clayton Act did little to remedy the defects of the Sherman Act.

The reasons for the watering down are several, but the most important was the outbreak of war in Europe that summer. The Wilson administration and the Congress did not want to do anything that would further demoralize the economy.[77] Brandeis recognized the reality of the political situation that summer, and in fact he and his close friend New York attorney George L. Rublee had drafted a bill in the spring that had been introduced by Representative Raymond B. Stevens of New Hampshire. The bill outlawed unfair trade practices in general rather than specific terms and then gave a new Federal Trade Commission the power to evaluate and rule on specific activities, with the authority to issue cease and desist orders to prevent the illegal suppression of competition. The Stevens bill had stalled in the House until the fall, when complaints arose that the Clayton bill had been too watered down. A strengthened Federal Trade Commission Act had been embraced by the administration as the way to save its antitrust policy, and with Wilson's backing it was passed by Congress in September.

THE CURSE OF BIGNESS

The Clayton Antitrust Act, as well as the Federal Trade Commission Act, failed to stop the drive toward bigness, and some commentators believe that Brandeis's views on the curse of bigness and the inefficiency of large corporations were naive at best and foolishly wrong at worst. The Federal Trade Commission, in Brandeis's view, was a failure from the start, when Wilson, for political reasons, named economic conservatives to the agency. Then during the Republican 1920s, the appointees of Presidents Harding, Coolidge, and Hoover actively opposed the very idea of government restricting business in any way and abandoned any effort to curb business abuses. By the time Franklin Roosevelt came to power, the Depression made it unlikely that the government would try to restrain business activity, and then World War II elevated production above all other considerations. In a number of ways, the Roosevelt administration actively promoted monopoly, such as in the National Industrial Recovery Act of 1933 and wartime price controls.

But one has to look at Brandeis's economic views in a larger context, namely, the relationship between private enterprise and the public good in a democratic state. The charges that Brandeis leveled in *Other People's Money* are not concerned simply with business abuses but with the effect such actions have on people and on the political system. Although he is writing in the guise of an economist, his real subjects are morality and political philosophy. Brandeis considered bigness immoral because of what it did to individual people. It deprived new entrepreneurs of opportunity by stifling the market. Bigness meant that the people nominally in charge of the industries had in fact no real control because they lacked the knowledge to run their businesses effectively (see chapter X). People had to have a sense of connection, of belonging, of having some importance in their jobs, and bigness deprived both the worker and the manager of these values. Beyond that, bigness subverted the political system by introducing a large and uncontrollable bloc of private power that could affect government far more than the unorganized wishes of the electorate could.[78] (See chapter VIII.) Not all Progressive reformers shared Brandeis's views about the immorality of bigness, but even those who, like Theodore Roosevelt, were prepared to accept bigness in industry feared the consequences of gigantic enterprises on the integrity of the political system. It is this aspect of Brandeis's thought that appealed to the widest range of reformers. Economists make many arguments about the virtues of big business, such as economies of size, efficiency in various operations, and even the fact that only large corporations can sustain major research and development functions. Many of Brandeis's contentions about the inefficiency of big business simply are not accurate, and there is some evidence that big corporations can and do provide an environment conducive to small entrepreneurs. Big companies do have privileged access to capital, but that is often a function of the achievements and past credit rating of the corporations, not merely of their size.

To Brandeis, any preferred credit constituted an unfair trade advantage and could be traced to the interlocking roles of banking and industrial interests. Moreover, only such unfair advantages made it possible for monopolies and other large corporations to survive. Worse, their inefficiencies, which should have allowed smaller and more able competitors to sweep the market, stood in the way of real competition, since the lords of finance would not grant credit to those who might compete successfully against the bloated giants. Such a system, Brandeis believed, perverted the market, threatened democracy, and in so doing sapped the moral energy of the nation. Even if one could have shown that big business could operate efficiently, Brandeis would still have argued that the moral and political systems of the country would have suffered. The problem, as he often said, was not monopoly but bigness itself. As far as the bankers were concerned, their greatest sin lay not in how they used their money to promote big business but in that they took no risk themselves; they did their work using other people's money.

THE "REFRESHING PERTINENCE" OF THE ARGUMENT

Throughout the 1920s Brandeis, whom Wilson had appointed to the Supreme Court in 1916, cast a baleful eye on the excesses of the business civilization over which the Republicans presided. The monopolies had distorted the marketplace by artificially maintaining high prices, and this had led to a situation in which big businesses had to produce more and more even as consumer demand fell. The Great Depression, while admittedly a tragedy for many innocent people, struck Brandeis as a just reward for those who had failed to heed the lessons he and other reformers had preached two decades earlier. "The present depression," he wrote to his nephew, "the debunking of the great financial kings, and the losses of those who followed them have made men think, and i.a. [*inter alia,* amongst themselves] realize that 'Other People's Money' should have been heeded."[79]

Convinced that the lessons of *Other People's Money* remained valid, Brandeis arranged for publication of an inexpensive edition in 1933 and noted with glee that a Washington department store sold over eleven hundred copies within one week.[80] Later in the Depression, Brandeis thought about having another edition printed, but by then recovery had started and foreign affairs had once again begun to crowd out economic reform as the focus of the nation's attention.

For the most part, economists have dismissed Brandeis's arguments about the inefficiency of big corporations, and many historians believe that nothing the New Freedom could have enacted would have turned the clock back to an era of small-unit business. In fact, the measures enacted in the Wilson years had little impact on industrial consolidation, a fact Brandeis noted and mourned. He believed that Roosevelt's New Deal had an opportunity to restructure the system, but he denounced the early New Deal, modeled on Theodore Roosevelt's New Nationalism, as the worst possible choice.

Rather, the structural reforms enacted from time to time have eliminated the worst abuses that Brandeis condemned, and laws currently on the books restrict bankers from engaging in many of the practices described in *Other People's Money.* The system, however, has continued to work, to provide jobs and goods and services, and that, as far as many people are concerned, is all that matters. The moral questions raised by Brandeis remain ignored for long periods of time until people are suddenly jolted back into an awareness that many of his concerns are still valid.

Thus the historian Richard M. Abrams, in his introduction to a 1967 edition of *Other People's Money,* wrote about the complacency with which most people viewed the continuing consolidation of economic power in a few hands. Defenders of the system maintained that the rate of consolidation had been stable for years, but Abrams noted that the concentration statistics

> tell us primarily about the intra-industrial shares of particular firms, but very little so far about inter-industrial influence by individual giants through a variety of relationships with subsidiaries, affiliates, and simply "friendly" corporate peers. DuPont's relationship with General Motors, its patent arrangements with Standard Oil, General Electric's ties to the electrical utilities, and the relationship of all the giants to the major

financial institutions, represent a degree of economy-wide control by a small segment of the "automatic self-perpetuating oligarchy."[81]

While *Other People's Money* remained primarily a document of Progressive era reform and "shows its age in the various weaknesses of its arguments," Abrams nonetheless concluded that "even for our time, now a half century later, only a willful reluctance to test fundamentals can obscure its refreshing pertinence."[82]

AN ENDURING LESSON

That "refreshing pertinence" is even more compelling after the excesses of the 1980s, many of which also stemmed from the ability of bankers to gamble with other people's money. The Republican administration either turned a blind eye to or actively encouraged the mania for mergers and leveraged buyouts. Financiers issued billions of dollars of so-called junk bonds to put together gigantic corporations and then sold off valuable assets to pay for the buyouts, bilking investors of tens of billions of dollars. Wall Street was as immoral as it had been in the days of "frenzied finance," with insiders using privileged information to make millions through advance purchases or sales. Law firms charged multimillion-dollar fees to help banks put together acquisitions with terribly fragile financial underpinnings.[83]

Perhaps worst of all, savings banks engaged in a frenzy of speculative financing. Small thrift institutions could be bought cheaply enough, and then the insured savings of their customers could be leveraged to finance enormous ventures in real estate. Brandeis had, in fact, opposed deposit insurance when it had been proposed in the 1930s for fear of just these abuses—that insured savings would lead bank officers to neglect their responsibilities to depositors, since insurance would cover all losses. He would also have been saddened by the behavior of savings and loan officials, since in the Progressive era he had held these bankers up as paragons, people who diligently managed their customers' money and faithfully served the interests of the community.[84] (See chapter X.) The failure of the thrifts, as well as the bankruptcies of so many of the leveraged mergers and buyouts in the 1990s, would not have surprised him, and he would have felt only scorn for the perpetrators.

It is one measure of how little progress has been made in this area that eight decades after its publication, the moral fervor of *Other People's Money* not only rings true but speaks in a contemporary manner as well.

NOTES

[1] This view was first articulated by Samuel P. Hays in *The Response to Industrialism, 1885–1914* (Chicago: University of Chicago Press, 1957) and was modified somewhat in Robert Wiebe, *The Search for Order, 1877–1920* (New York: Hill & Wang, 1967).

[2] The role of business leaders in seeking to rationalize the economy through legislation was first noted in Gabriel Kolko, *The Triumph of Conservatism* (New York: Free Press, 1963), and Wiebe's *Search for Order* expanded on the role of middle-class businesspeople in reform. Kolko downplayed the democratic nature of Progressive reform, but other scholars have defended the democratic nature of reform; see John P. Buenker, *Urban Liberalism and Progressive Reform* (New York: Scribner's, 1973), and David P. Thelen, *The New Citizenship* (Columbia, Mo.: University of Missouri Press, 1972).

[3] Peter Filene, in "An Obituary for 'The Progressive Movement,'" *American Quarterly* 22 (Spring 1970): 20, argues that there was no Progressive movement; see, however, the response by Daniel Rodgers, "In Search of Progressivism," *Reviews in American History* 10 (1982): 113.

[4] The clearest expression of Roosevelt's ideas can be found in a speech he gave at Osawatomie, Kansas, on September 1, 1910; see Theodore Roosevelt, *The New Nationalism* (New York: Outlook Company, 1911), 3–33.

[5] For Brandeis's life, see Philippa Strum, *Louis D. Brandeis: Justice for the People* (Cambridge: Harvard University Press, 1984); Alpheus T. Mason, *Brandeis: A Free Man's Life* (New York: Viking, 1946); and Melvin I. Urofsky, *A Mind of One Piece: Brandeis and American Reform* (New York: Scribner's, 1971).

[6] Brandeis to Amy Brandeis Wehle, January 20, 1877, in Melvin I. Urofsky and David W. Levy, eds., *Letters of Louis D. Brandeis*, 5 vols. (Albany: State University of New York Press, 1971–1978) 1:14. Hereafter cited as *Brandeis Letters*.

[7] James Willard Hurst, *The Growth of American Law: The Law Makers* (Boston: Little, Brown, 1950), 345.

[8] Oliver Wendell Holmes, Jr., "The Path of the Law," *Collected Legal Papers* (New York: Harcourt, Brace & Howe, 1920), 187.

[9] See the recollections of his law partner, Edward F. McClennan, "Louis D. Brandeis as a Lawyer," *Massachusetts Law Quarterly* 33 (1948): 1. See also Strum, *Brandeis*, chap. 2, and Urofsky, *Mind of One Piece*, chap. 2.

[10] *Boston Herald*, June 20, 1905.

[11] Edward A. Filene, "Louis D. Brandeis as We Know Him," *Boston Post*, July 14, 1915.

[12] *Current Literature* (March 1911), cited in Alfred Lief, ed., *The Brandeis Guide to the Modern World* (Boston: Little, Brown, 1941), 38.

[13] At a time when most lawyers in the country made less than $5,000 a year, Brandeis's annual income exceeded $50,000. He lived simply and invested cautiously but wisely, so that by 1907 his net worth exceeded one million dollars. By the time he went onto the Supreme Court in 1916, that figure had doubled, even though he had all but given up the active practice of law by 1913.

[14] This idea is eloquently expressed in Justice Brandeis's concurring opinion in *Whitney v. California*, 274 U.S. 357, 374 (1927).

[15] For a case study of the fight for savings bank life insurance, see Alpheus T. Mason, *The Brandeis Way* (Princeton: Princeton University Press, 1938).

[16] Interview with Elizabeth Brandeis Raushenbush.

[17] *Muller v. Oregon*, 208 U.S. 412 (1908).

[18] For a survey of protective legislation in the courts, see Melvin I. Urofsky, "Myth and Reality: The Supreme Court and Protective Legislation in the Progressive Era," *Yearbook of the Supreme Court Historical Society* (1983): 53–72, and "State Courts and Protective Legislation in the Progressive Era: A Reevaluation," *Journal of American History* 72 (1985): 63–91.

[19] *Lochner v. New York*, 198 U.S. 45 (1905).

[20] Quoted in Mason, *Brandeis*, 248–49.

[21] The brief is reprinted as *Women in Industry . . . Brief for the State of Oregon* (New York: Consumers League, 1908). For the compiling of the brief, see Josephine Goldmark, *Impatient Crusader: Florence Kelley's Life Story* (Urbana: University of Illinois Press, 1953).

[22] 208 U.S. at 421.

[23] On scientific management, see Frederick W. Taylor, *Principles of Scientific Management* (New York: Harper & Brothers, 1911), and Frank B. Gilbreth, *Primer of Scientific Management* (New York: Van Nostrand, 1914).

[24] Philippa Strum, *Brandeis: Beyond Progressivism* (Lawrence: University Press of Kansas, 1993), 43–45; Oscar Kraines, "Brandeis' Philosophy of Scientific Management," *Western Political Quarterly* 13 (1960): 191.

[25] Strum, *Brandeis: Beyond Progressivism*, 45.

[26] Mason, *Brandeis*, chaps. 20, 21.

[27] The entire story of the controversy is told in Alpheus T. Mason, *Bureaucracy Convicts Itself* (New York: 1941), and from a much different perspective in James L. Penick, Jr., *Progressive Politics and Conservation: The Ballinger-Pinchot Affair* (Chicago: University of Chicago Press, 1968). See also Samuel P. Hays, *Conservation and the Gospel of Efficiency* (Cambridge: Harvard University Press, 1959).

[28] For details, see Mason, *Brandeis*, chap. 19; Strum, *Brandeis*, 174ff.

[29] This issue is explored at length in Melvin I. Urofsky, *American Zionism from Herzl to the Holocaust* (Garden City: Doubleday, 1975); see also Strum, *Brandeis: Beyond Progressivism*, 100–115.

[30] The story of the nomination fight is well told in Mason, *Brandeis*, chaps. 30 and 31, and Alden L. Todd, *Justice on Trial* (New York: McGraw-Hill, 1964).

[31] The most explicit statement of this view is in Brandeis's dissent in *New State Ice Co. v. Liebman*, 285 U.S. 262, 287 (1932).

[32] *Gilbert v. Minnesota*, 254 U.S. 325, 343 (1920) (dissenting).

[33] *Schenck v. United States*, 249 U.S. 47 (1919).

[34] *Whitney v. California*, 274 U.S. 357, 372 (1927) (concurring). For a brilliant explication of the Brandeis opinion, see Vincent Blasi, "The First Amendment and the Ideal of Civil Courage: The Brandeis Opinion in *Whitney v. California*," *William and Mary Law Review* 29 (1988): 653.

[35] The most extensive "exposé" of Brandeis's extrajudicial activities is Bruce A. Murphy, *The Brandeis/Frankfurter Connection* (New York: Oxford University Press, 1982); for a more balanced view of Brandeis's activities in the light of then-prevailing judicial ethics, see David J. Danelski, "The Propriety of Brandeis's Extrajudicial Conduct," in Nelson L. Dawson, ed., *Brandeis and America* (Lexington: University Press of Kentucky, 1989).

[36] The New Haven story is told from a viewpoint sympathetic to Brandeis in Henry Lee Staples and Alpheus T. Mason, *The Fall of a Railroad Empire: Brandeis and the New Haven Merger Battle* (Syracuse: Syracuse University Press, 1947). A different perspective can be found in Richard M. Abrams, *Conservatism in a Progressive Era: Massachusetts Politics, 1900–1912* (Cambridge: Harvard University Press, 1964), chap. 8.

[37] Brandeis to Norman Hapgood, February 27, 1911, in *Brandeis Letters* 2:412.

[38] *Boston American*, December 14, 1911.

[39] *Other People's Money*, 19.

[40] John Moody, *The Truth about the Trusts* (New York: Moody Publishing Co., 1904). More recent scholarly studies have placed the figure somewhat higher, at 257 new combinations between 1897 and 1904; in any event, all are agreed that the rate of consolidation proceeded at a frenetic pace at the turn of the century.

[41] Moody, *Truth about Trusts*, 492–93.

[42] Louis D. Brandeis, "Our New Peonage: Discretionary Pensions," *The Independent*, July 25, 1912, 187.

[43] This idea, as well as Brandeis's views on a variety of social and political issues, is explored in Strum, *Brandeis: Beyond Progressivism.*

[44] Senate Committee on Interstate Commerce, *Hearings on Control of Corporations, Persons, and Firms Engaged in Interstate Commerce,* 62nd Cong., 2nd sess. (Washington: Government Printing Office, 1911).

[45] Lief, *Brandeis Guide,* 124.

[46] Testimony before the U.S. Commission on Industrial Relations, reprinted in Osmund K. Fraenkel, ed., *The Curse of Bigness: Miscellaneous Papers of Louis D. Brandeis* (New York: Viking, 1934), 81.

[47] Theodore Roosevelt, "The Trusts, the People, and the Square Deal," *The Outlook,* November 18, 1911, 649.

[48] John Wells Davidson, ed., *A Crossroads of Freedom: The 1912 Campaign Speeches of Woodrow Wilson* (New Haven: Yale University Press, 1956), 79, 113, 171.

[49] "Suggestions for Letter of Governor Wilson on Trusts," enclosed in Brandeis to Wilson, September 30, 1912, *Brandeis Letters* 2:688.

[50] Companies that wanted to raise cash to expand their plants often issued new stock; that was, and remains, an accepted method for raising capital. "Manufactured securities" refers to stock issued to finance mergers and raise the money to pay legal and brokerage fees. The new stock does not add anything to the value of the company and in fact devalues existing shares. In the 1990s, we might use the term "manufactured securities" to refer to junk bonds and stock issues to cover the cost of leveraged buyouts and mergers.

[51] Quoted in *Literary Digest,* January 4, 1913, 388.

[52] Ray Stannard Baker and William E. Dodd, eds., *The Public Papers of Woodrow Wilson,* 6 vols. (New York: Harper & Brothers, 1925–27), 1:6.

[53] From 1791 until 1913, the federal government did not issue paper currency (with the single exception of the so-called greenback notes during the Civil War) but minted only gold and silver coins. Private banks issued "bank notes," which circulated as currency and were backed by the reserves of the bank issuing them. In hard times, if a bank went under, its notes lost all value, and people holding those notes had nothing left but pieces of worthless paper.

[54] George E. Mowry, *The Era of Theodore Roosevelt and the Birth of Modern America, 1900–1912* (New York: Harper & Row, 1958), 216–19. In addition, at the behest of J. P. Morgan, Roosevelt approved the purchase of the Tennessee Coal and Iron Company by the U.S. Steel Corporation in order to stave off the collapse of a major brokerage firm, whose failure, according to Morgan, would have had serious repercussions throughout the banking community.

[55] Commercial paper consists of notes and bonds issued by corporations, which are considered to have a greater value than private notes. Currency based on commercial paper would, in effect, rely on the credit worthiness of the corporations issuing that paper.

[56] *Report . . . of the National Monetary Commission,* Senate doc. 243, 62nd Cong., 2nd sess. (Washington: Government Printing Office, 1912). For an analysis of the banking system at this time and the development of various plans leading up to the Wilsonian reforms, see H. Parker Willis, *The Federal Reserve System* (New York: Ronald Press, 1923).

[57] Arthur S. Link, *Woodrow Wilson and the Progressive Era, 1910–1917* (New York: Harper & Row, 1954), 46–47.

[58] Brandeis to Untermyer, March 8, 1913, quoted in Mason, *Brandeis,* 412. Untermyer agreed and explained that because of time constraints the committee had been unable to call all the witnesses it wanted to examine, and he himself had to write the report in less than ten days.

[59] See, for example, Brandeis to John M. Walton, August 1, 1913, in *Brandeis Letters* 3:159, seeking information on how the city of Philadelphia placed its bond issues.

[60] Alfred Lief, *Brandeis: The Personal History of an American Ideal* (New York: Stackpole, 1936), 205.

[61] Brandeis to Wilson, June 14, 1913, in *Brandeis Letters* 3:113.

[62] These challenges included raising, training, and maintaining an army of several million men and organizing the economy to deliver the materials of war, tasks that could be undertaken only by a strong central government. For details, see Robert D. Cuff, *The War Industries Board: Business-Government Relations during World War I* (Baltimore: Johns Hopkins University Press, 1973).

[63] Brandeis had published many of his earlier articles in *Collier's Weekly* and had in fact been counsel for the magazine in the 1911 Pinchot-Ballinger hearings. But during the 1912 campaign, relations between the publisher, Robert Collier, and the editor, Norman Hapgood, had grown increasingly strained, with Hapgood backing Wilson and Collier supporting Roosevelt. Collier fired Hapgood on October 14, 1912, and after the election Hapgood, with Brandeis's help, assumed editorial control of *Harper's Weekly.*

When one reader asked Brandeis why he did not publish his articles in a journal with larger circulation, such as the *Saturday Evening Post*, Brandeis replied that several people had made this suggestion, but "I regard Mr. Hapgood as so important a factor in the American advance movement that if I have been of any service in helping *Harper's Weekly*, as his instrument, I shall feel well content with the decision made." Brandeis to Joseph R. Smith, February 2, 1914, in *Brandeis Letters* 3:243.

[64] The published edition included a tenth article, "The Failure of Banker-Management," which Brandeis had published in *Harper's* in August 1913. Both Hapgood and Frederick A. Stokes, who published the articles in book form, wanted the book entitled *Every Man's Money and What the Bankers Do with It*, but Brandeis preferred *Other People's Money*. Brandeis may well have been familiar with Adam Smith's charge that "the directors of companies, . . . being the managers rather of other people's money than of their own, it cannot well be expected, that they should watch over it with the same anxious vigilance with which partners . . . frequently watch over their own."

[65] Opinion on the articles and book can be found in Mason, *Brandeis*, 418–19.

[66] *Other People's Money*, 92.

[67] The work of Tarbell, Baker, and Steffens is examined in Ellen F. Fitzpatrick, *Muckraking: Three Landmark Articles* (Boston: Bedford, 1994).

[68] Philippa Strum, in *Brandeis: Beyond Progressivism*, suggests that Brandeis was more concerned with securing industrial democracy that would, at least in part, level the playing field in favor of the workers.

[69] Ray Stannard Baker, *Woodrow Wilson: Life and Letters*, 8 vols. (Garden City: Doubleday, 1927–39), 3:432.

[70] David Houston, *Eight Years with Wilson's Cabinet*, 2 vols. (Garden City: Doubleday, 1926), 1:85–86; H. L. Higginson to Wilson, December 19, 1913, Woodrow Wilson Papers, Library of Congress.

[71] Brandeis to Franklin K. Lane, December 12, 1913, *Brandeis Letters* 3:221.

[72] Brandeis later changed his mind on this and convinced Wilson that the Federal Trade Commission should have regulatory powers; see Urofsky, *Mind of One Piece*, 89–91.

[73] Baker and Dodd, *Public Papers* 3:81–88.

[74] Brandeis to Alfred Brandeis, January 23, 1913; for the ideas at the "first interview," see Brandeis to Wilson, September 30, 1912, *Brandeis Letters* 3:686–94.

[75] Senate Committee on Interstate Commerce, *Hearings on Interstate Trade*, 63rd Cong., 2nd sess. (Washington, 1914), 947–67.

[76] Link, *Wilson and the Progressive Movement*, 72–73.

[77] For example, the Rayburn bill, which would have given the Interstate Commerce Commission control over the issuance of new stocks and bonds by the railroads, had passed the House of Representatives in early June 1914. Following the outbreak of war, however, the American securities markets were in panic condition; the New York Stock Exchange closed for a period, and some railroads verged on bankruptcy since they could not find purchasers for new securities. To reassure business leaders, the administration agreed to kill the Rayburn bill.

[78] David W. Levy, "Brandeis and the Progressive Movement," in Dawson, ed., *Brandeis and America*, 109.

[79] Brandeis to Louis B. Wehle, January 19, 1932, *Brandeis Letters* 5:494.

[80] Brandeis to Sherman Mittell, August 25, 1933, *Brandeis Letters* 5:519; Brandeis to Felix Frankfurter, December 17, 1933, in Melvin I. Urofsky and David W. Levy, eds., *"Half Brother, Half Son": The Letters of Louis D. Brandeis to Felix Frankfurter* (Norman: University of Oklahoma Press, 1991), 536.

[81] Richard M. Abrams, introduction to Louis D. Brandeis, *Other People's Money* (New York: Harper & Row, 1967), xlii.

[82] Ibid., xliv.

[83] See, among many books on the sharp practices of the 1980s, Michael M. Lewis, *Liar's Poker: Rising through the Wreckage on Wall Street* (New York: Norton, 1989), and Bryan Burrough and John Helyar, *Barbarians at the Gate: The Fall of RJR Nabisco* (New York: Harper & Row, 1990).

[84] Brandeis described the trustees and officers of savings banks as men "who had been trained to recognize that the business of investing the savings of persons of small means is a quasi-public trust which should be conducted as a beneficent and not as a selfish money-making institution." "Wage-Earners' Life Insurance," *Collier's Weekly*, September 15, 1906, 16ff., reprinted in *Business: A Profession* (Boston: Small, Maynard, 1914), 174.

PART TWO

The Document

Other People's Money and How the Bankers Use It by Louis D. Brandeis

Preface

While Louis D. Brandeis's series of articles on the money trust was running in *Harper's Weekly* many inquiries came about publication in more accessible permanent form. Even without such urgence through the mail, however, it would have been clear that these articles inevitably constituted a book, since they embodied an analysis and a narrative by that mind which, on the great industrial movements of our era, is the most expert in the United States. The inquiries meant that the attentive public recognized that here was a contribution to history. Here was the clearest and most profound treatment ever published on that part of our business development which, as President Wilson and other wise men have said, has come to constitute the greatest of our problems. The story of our time is the story of industry. No scholar of the future will be able to describe our era with authority unless he comprehends that expansion and concentration which followed the harnessing of steam and electricity, the great uses of the change, and the great excesses. No historian of the future, in my opinion, will find among our contemporary documents so masterful an analysis of why concentration went astray. I am but one among many who look upon Mr. Brandeis as having, in the field of economics, the most inventive and sound mind of our time. While his articles were running in *Harper's Weekly* I had ample opportunity to know how widespread was the belief among intelligent men that this brilliant diagnosis of our money trust was the most important contribution to current thought in many years.

"Great" is one of the words that I do not use loosely, and I look upon Mr. Brandeis as a great man. In the composition of his intellect, one of the most important elements is his comprehension of figures. As one of the leading financiers of the country said to me, "Mr. Brandeis's greatness as a lawyer is part of his greatness as a mathematician." My views on this subject are sufficiently indicated in the following editorial in *Harper's Weekly*.

ARITHMETIC

About five years before the Metropolitan Traction Company of New York went into the hands of a receiver, Mr. Brandeis came down from Boston, and in a speech at Cooper Union prophesied that that company must fail. Leading bankers in New York and Boston were heartily recommending the stock to their customers. Mr. Brandeis made his prophecy merely by analyzing the published figures. How did he win in the Pinchot-Glavis-Ballinger controversy? In various ways, no doubt; but perhaps the most critical step was when he calculated just how long it would take a fast worker to go through the Glavis-Ballinger record and make a judgment of it; whereupon he decided that Mr. Wickersham* could not have made his report at the time it was stated to have been made, and therefore it must have been predated.

Most of Mr. Brandeis's other contributions to current history have involved arithmetic. When he succeeded in preventing a raise in freight rates, it was through an exact analysis of cost. When he got Savings Bank Insurance started in Massachusetts, it was by being able to figure what insurance ought to cost. When he made the best contract between a city and a public utility that exists in this country, a definite grasp of the gas business was necessary—combined, of course, with the wisdom and originality that make a statesman. He could not have invented the preferential shop if that new idea had not been founded on a precise knowledge of the conditions in the garment trades. When he established before the United States Supreme Court the constitutionality of legislation affecting women only, he relied much less upon reason than upon the amount of knowledge displayed of what actually happens to women when they are overworked—which, while not arithmetic, is built on the same intellectual quality. Nearly two years before Mr. Mellen resigned [as president of] the New Haven Railroad, Mr. Brandeis wrote to the present editor of this paper a private letter in which he said:

> When the New Haven reduces its dividends and Mellen resigns, the "Decline of New Haven and Fall of Mellen" will make a dramatic story of human interest with a moral—or two—including the evils of private monopoly. Events cannot be long deferred, and possibly you may want to prepare for their coming.
>
> Anticipating the future a little, I suggest the following as an epitaph or obituary notice:

* *George W. Wickersham*, a New York attorney, served as attorney general in the Taft administration.

Mellen was a masterful man, resourceful, courageous, broad of view. He fired the imagination of New England; but, being oblique of vision, merely distorted its judgment and silenced its conscience. For a while he trampled with impunity on laws human and divine; but, as he was obsessed with the delusion that two and two make five, he fell, at last, a victim to the relentless rules of humble arithmetic. "Remember, O Stranger, Arithmetic is the first of the sciences and the mother of safety."

The exposure of the bad financial management of the New Haven railroad, more than any other one thing, led to the exposure and comprehension of the wasteful methods of big business all over the country and that exposure of the New Haven was the almost single-handed work of Mr. Brandeis. He is a person who fights against any odds while it is necessary to fight and stops fighting as soon as the fight is won. For a long time very respectable and honest leaders of finance said that his charges against the New Haven were unsound and inexcusable. He kept ahead. A year before the actual crash came, however, he ceased worrying, for he knew the work had been carried far enough to complete itself. When someone asked him to take part in some little controversy shortly before the collapse, he replied, "That fight does not need me any longer. Time and arithmetic will do the rest."

This grasp of the concrete is combined in Mr. Brandeis with an equally distinguished grasp of bearing and significance. His imagination is as notable as his understanding of business. In those accomplishments which have given him his place in American life, the two sides of his mind have worked together. The arrangement between the Gas Company and the City of Boston rests on one of the guiding principles of Mr. Brandeis's life, that no contract is good that is not advantageous to both parties to it. Behind his understanding of the methods of obtaining insurance and the proper cost of it to the laboring man lay a philosophy of the vast advantage to the fiber and energy of the community that would come from devising methods by which the laboring classes could make themselves comfortable through their whole lives and thus perhaps making unnecessary elaborate systems of state help. The most important ideas put forth in the Armstrong Committee* Report on insurance had been previously suggested by Mr. Brandeis, acting as counsel for the Equitable policy holders. Business and the more important statesmanship were intimately combined in the management of the Protocol in New York, which has done so much to

* In 1905 the New York legislature, at the behest of Governor Frank W. Higgins, launched an investigation into abuses and corruption in the insurance industry. The investigating committee was called the *Armstrong Committee* after its chair, Senator William W. Armstrong.

improve conditions in the clothing industry. The welfare of the laborer and his relation to his employer seems to Mr. Brandeis, as it does to all the most competent thinkers today, to constitute the most important question we have to solve, and he won the case, coming up to the Supreme Court of the United States, from Oregon, establishing the constitutionality of special protective legislation for women. In the Minimum Wage case, also from the State of Oregon, which is about to be heard before the Supreme Court, he takes up what is really a logical sequence of the limitation of women's hours in certain industries, since it would be a futile performance to limit their hours and then allow their wages to be cut down in consequence. These industrial activities are in large part an expression of his deep and ever growing sympathy with the working people and understanding of them. Florence Kelley once said: "No man since Lincoln has understood the common people as Louis Brandeis does."

While the majority of Mr. Brandeis's great progressive achievements have been connected with the industrial system, some have been political in a more limited sense. I worked with him through the Ballinger-Pinchot controversy, and I never saw a grasp of detail more brilliantly combined with high constructive ethical and political thinking. After the man who knew most about the details of the Interior Department had been cross-examined by Mr. Brandeis he came and sat down by me and said: "Mr. Hapgood, I have no respect for you. I do not think your motives in this agitation are good motives, but I want to say that you have a wonderful lawyer. He knows as much about the Interior Department today as I do." In that controversy, the power of the administration and of the ruling forces in the House and Senate were combined to protect Secretary Ballinger and prevent the truth from coming to light. Mr. Brandeis, in leading the fight for the conservation side, was constantly haunted by the idea that there was a mystery somewhere. The editorial printed above hints at how he solved the mystery, but it would require much more space to tell the other sides, the enthusiasm for conservation, the convincing arguments for higher standards in office, the connection of this conspiracy with the country's larger needs. Seldom is an audience at a hearing so moved as it was by Mr. Brandeis's final plea to the committee.

Possibly his work on railroads will turn out to be the most significant among the many things Mr. Brandeis has done. His arguments in 1910–11 before the Interstate Commerce Commission against the raising of rates, on the ground that the way for railroads to be more prosperous was to be more efficient, made efficiency a national idea. It is a cardinal point in his philosophy that the only real progress toward a higher national life will come through efficiency in all our activities. The seventy-eight questions addressed to the railroads by the Interstate Commerce Commission in

December, 1913, embody what is probably the most comprehensive embodiment of his thought on the subject.

On nothing has he ever worked harder than on his diagnosis of the Money Trust, and when his life comes to be written (I hope many years hence) this will be ranked with his railroad work for its effect in accelerating industrial changes. It is indeed more than a coincidence that so many of the things he has been contending for have come to pass. It is seldom that one man puts one idea, not to say many ideas, effectively before the world, but it is no exaggeration to say that Mr. Brandeis is responsible for the now widespread recognition of the inherent weakness of great size. He was the first person who set forth effectively the doctrine that there is a limit to the size of greatest efficiency, and the successful demonstration of that truth is a profound contribution to the subject of trusts. The demonstration is powerfully put in his testimony before the Senate Committee in 1911, and it is powerfully put in this volume. In destroying the delusion that efficiency was a common incident of size, he emphasized the possibility of efficiency through intensive development of the individual, thus connecting this principle with his whole study of efficiency, and pointing the way to industrial democracy.

Not less notable than the intellect and the constructive ability that have gone into Mr. Brandeis's work are the exceptional moral qualities. Any powerful and entirely sincere crusader must sacrifice much. Mr. Brandeis has sacrificed much in money, in agreeableness of social life, in effort, and he has done it for principle and for human happiness. His power of intensive work, his sustained interest and will, and his courage have been necessary for leadership. No man could have done what he has done without being willing to devote his life to making his dreams come true.

Nor should anyone make the mistake, because the labors of Mr. Brandeis and others have recently brought about changes, that the system which was being attacked has been undermined. The currency bill has been passed, and as these words are written, it looks as if a group of trust bills would be passed. But systems are not ended in a day. Of the truths which are embodied in the essays printed in this book, some are being carried out now, but it will be many, many years before the whole idea can be made effective; and there will, therefore, be many, many years during which active citizens will be struggling for those principles which are here so clearly, so eloquently, so conclusively set forth.

The articles reprinted here were all written before November, 1913. "The Failure of Banker Management" appeared in *Harper's Weekly* Aug. 16, 1913; the other articles, between Nov. 22, 1913 and Jan. 17, 1914.

Norman Hapgood

March, 1914

Contents

Chapter I

Our Financial Oligarchy

President Wilson, when Governor, declared in 1911:

The great monopoly in this country is the money monopoly. So long as that exists, our old variety and freedom and individual energy of development are out of the question. A great industrial nation is controlled by its system of credit. Our system of credit is concentrated. The growth of the nation, therefore, and all our activities are in the hands of a few men, who, even if their actions be honest and intended for the public interest, are necessarily concentrated upon the great undertakings in which their own money is involved and who, necessarily, by every reason of their own limitations, chill and check and destroy genuine economic freedom. This is the greatest question of all; and to this, statesmen must address themselves with an earnest determination to serve the long future and the true liberties of men.

The Pujo Committee—appointed in 1912—found:

Far more dangerous than all that has happened to us in the past in the way of elimination of competition in industry is the control of credit through the domination of these groups over our banks and industries. . . .

Whether under a different currency system the resources in our banks would be greater or less is comparatively immaterial if they continue to be controlled by a small group. . . .

It is impossible that there should be competition with all the facilities for raising money or selling large issues of bonds in the hands of these few bankers and their partners and allies, who together dominate the financial policies of most of the existing systems. . . . The acts of this inner group, as here described, have nevertheless been more destructive of competition than anything accomplished by the trusts, for they strike at the very vitals of potential competition in every industry that is under their protection, a condition which if permitted to continue, will render impossible all attempts to restore normal competitive conditions in the industrial world. . . .

If the arteries of credit now clogged well-nigh to choking by the obstructions created through the control of these groups are opened so that they may be permitted freely to play their important part in the financial system, competition in large enterprises will become possible and business can be conducted on its merits instead of being subject to the tribute and the good will of this handful of self-constituted trustees of the national prosperity.

The promise of New Freedom was joyously proclaimed in 1913. The facts which the Pujo Investigating Committee and its able Counsel, Mr. Samuel Untermyer, have laid before the country, show clearly the means by which a few men control the business of America. The report proposes measures which promise some relief. Additional remedies will be proposed. Congress will soon be called upon to act. How shall the emancipation be wrought? On what lines shall we proceed? The facts, when fully understood, will teach us.

The Dominant Element

The dominant element in our financial oligarchy is the investment banker. Associated banks, trust companies and life insurance companies are his tools. Controlled railroads, public service and industrial corporations are his subjects. Though properly but middlemen, these bankers bestride as masters America's business world, so that practically no large enterprise can be undertaken successfully without their participation or approval. These bankers are, of course, able men possessed of large fortunes; but the most potent factor in their control of business is not the possession of extraordinary ability or huge wealth. The key to their power is Combination—concentration intensive and comprehensive—advancing on three distinct lines:

First: There is the obvious consolidation of banks and trust companies; the less obvious affiliations—through stockholdings, voting trusts, and interlocking directorates—of banking institutions which are not legally connected; and the joint transactions, gentlemen's agreements, and "banking ethics" which eliminate competition among the investment bankers.

Second: There is the consolidation of railroads into huge systems, the large combinations of public service corporations, and the formation of industrial trusts, which, by making businesses so "big" that local, independent banking concerns cannot alone supply the necessary funds, has created dependence upon the associated New York bankers.

But combination, however intensive, along these lines only, could not have produced the Money Trust—another and more potent factor of combination was added.

Third: Investment bankers, like J. P. Morgan & Co., dealers in bonds, stocks, and notes, encroached upon the functions of the three other classes of corporations with which their business brought them into contact. They became the directing power in railroads, public service, and industrial companies through which our great business operations are conducted—the makers of bonds and stocks. They became the directing power in the life insurance companies, and other corporate reservoirs of the people's savings—the buyers of bonds and stocks. They became the directing power also in banks and trust companies—the depositaries of the quick capital of the country—the life blood of business, with which they and others carried on their operations. Thus four distinct functions, each essential to business, and each exercised, originally, by a distinct set of men, became united in the investment banker. It is to this union of business functions that the existence of the Money Trust is mainly due.*

The development of our financial oligarchy followed, in this respect, lines with which the history of political despotism has familiarized us:— usurpation, proceeding by gradual encroachment rather than by violent acts; subtle and often long-concealed concentration of distinct functions, which are beneficent when separately administered, and dangerous only when combined in the same persons. It was by processes such as these that Caesar Augustus became master of Rome. The makers of our own Constitution had in mind like dangers to our political liberty when they provided so carefully for the separation of governmental powers.

The Proper Sphere of the Investment Banker

The original function of the investment banker was that of dealer in bonds, stocks, and notes; buying mainly at wholesale from corporations, municipalities, states, and governments which need money, and selling to those seeking investments. The banker performs, in this respect, the function of a merchant; and the function is a very useful one. Large business enterprises are conducted generally by corporations. The permanent capital of corporations is represented by bonds and stocks. The bonds and stocks of the more important corporations are owned, in large part, by small investors, who do not participate in the management of the company. Corporations require the aid of a banker-middleman, for they lack generally the reputation and clientele essential to selling their own bonds and stocks direct to the investor. Investors in corporate securities, also, require the services of a banker-middleman. The number of securities upon the market is very large. Only a part of these securities is listed on the New York Stock Exchange; but its listings alone comprise about

---

* Obviously only a few of the investment bankers exercise this great power; but many others perform important functions in the system; as hereinafter described. [Brandeis's note]

sixteen hundred different issues aggregating about $26,500,000,000, and each year new listings are made averaging about two hundred and thirty-three to an amount of $1,500,000,000. For a small investor to make an intelligent selection from these many corporate securities—indeed, to pass an intelligent judgment upon a single one—is ordinarily impossible. He lacks the ability, the facilities, the training, and the time essential to a proper investigation. Unless his purchase is to be little better than a gamble, he needs the advice of an expert, who, combining special knowledge with judgment, has the facilities and incentive to make a thorough investigation. This dependence, both of corporations and of investors, upon the banker has grown in recent years, since women and others who do not participate in the management, have become the owners of so large a part of the stocks and bonds of our great corporations. Over half of the stockholders of the American Sugar Refining Company and nearly half of the stockholders of the Pennsylvania Railroad and of the New York, New Haven & Hartford Railroad are women.

Good-will—the possession by a dealer of numerous and valuable regular customers—is always an important element in merchandising. But in the business of selling bonds and stocks, it is of exceptional value, for the very reason that the small investor relies so largely upon the banker's judgment. This confidential relation of the banker to customers—and the knowledge of the customers' private affairs acquired incidentally—is often a determining factor in the marketing of securities. With the advent of Big Business such good-will possessed by the older banking houses, pre-eminently J. P. Morgan & Co. and their Philadelphia House called Drexel & Co., by Lee, Higginson & Co. and Kidder, Peabody, & Co. of Boston, and by Kuhn, Loeb & Co. of New York, became of enhanced importance. The volume of new security issues was greatly increased by huge railroad consolidations, the development of the holding companies, and particularly by the formation of industrial trusts. The rapidly accumulating savings of our people sought investment. The field of operations for the dealer in securities was thus much enlarged. And, as the securities were new and untried, the services of the investment banker were in great demand, and his powers and profits increased accordingly.

Controlling the Security Makers

But this enlargement of their legitimate field of operations did not satisfy investment bankers. They were not content merely to deal in securities. They desired to manufacture them also. They became promoters, or allied themselves with promoters. Thus it was that J. P. Morgan & Company formed the Steel Trust, the Harvester Trust and the Shipping Trust.* And, adding the duties of undertaker to those of midwife, the investment bankers became, in times of corporate disaster, members of security-holders' "Protective Committees"; then they participated as "Reorganization Managers" in the reincarnation of the unsuccessful corporations and ultimately became directors. It was in this way that the Morgan associates acquired their hold upon the Southern Railway, the Northern Pacific, the Reading, the Erie, the Père Marquette, the Chicago and Great Western, and the Cincinnati, Hamilton & Dayton. Often they insured the continuance of such control by the device of the voting trust;** but even where no voting trust was created, a secure hold was acquired upon reorganization. It was in this way also that Kuhn, Loeb & Co. became potent in the Union Pacific and in the Baltimore & Ohio.

But the banker's participation in the management of corporations was not limited to cases of promotion or reorganization. An urgent or extensive need of new money was considered a sufficient reason for the banker's entering a board of directors. Often without even such excuse the investment banker has secured a place upon the Board of Directors, through his powerful influence or the control of his customers' proxies. Such seems to have been the fatal entrance of Mr. Morgan into the management of the then prosperous New York, New Haven & Hartford Railroad, in 1892. When once a banker has entered the Board—whatever may have been the occasion—his grip proves tenacious and his influence usually supreme; for he controls the supply of new money.

The investment banker is naturally on the lookout for good bargains in bonds and stocks. Like other merchants, he wants to buy his merchandise cheap. But when he becomes director of a corporation, he occupies a position which prevents the transaction by which he acquires its corporate securities from being properly called a bargain. Can there be real bargaining where the same man is on both sides of a trade? The investment banker, through his controlling influence on the Board of Directors, decides that the corporation shall issue and sell the securities, decides the price at which it shall sell them, and decides that it shall sell the securities to himself. The fact that there are other directors besides the banker on

* The *Harvester Trust* and the *Shipping Trust* had been put together by the Morgan bank, and each combined several previously competing companies into a larger consolidation that dominated the industry.

** A *voting trust* was one in which the constituent companies had a vote on the board of trustees; a nonvoting trust was one in which the trustees were appointed by the banks and were self-perpetuating.

the Board does not, in practice, prevent this being the result. The banker, who holds the purse-strings, becomes usually the dominant spirit. Through voting-trusteeships, exclusive financial agencies, membership on executive or finance committees, or by mere directorships, J. P. Morgan & Co., and their associates, held such financial power in at least thirty-two transportation systems, public utility corporations, and industrial companies—companies with an aggregate capitalization of $17,273,000,000. Mainly for corporations so controlled, J. P. Morgan & Co. procured the public marketing in ten years of security issues aggregating $1,950,000,000. This huge sum does not include any issues marketed privately, nor any issues, however marketed, of intra-state corporations. Kuhn, Loeb & Co. and a few other investment bankers exercise similar control over many other corporations.

Controlling Security Buyers

Such control of railroads, public service, and industrial corporations assures to the investment bankers an ample supply of securities at attractive prices; and merchandise well bought is half sold. But these bond and stock merchants are not disposed to take even a slight risk as to their ability to market their goods. They saw that if they could control the security-buyers, as well as the security-makers, investment banking would, indeed, be "a happy hunting ground"; and they have made it so.

The numerous small investors cannot, in the strict sense, be controlled; but their dependence upon the banker insures their being duly influenced. A large part, however, of all bonds issued and of many stocks are bought by the prominent corporate investors; and most prominent among these are the life insurance companies, the trust companies, and the banks. The purchase of a security by these institutions not only relieves the banker of the merchandise, but recommends it strongly to the small investor, who believes that these institutions are wisely managed. These controlled corporate investors are not only large customers, but may be particularly accommodating ones. Individual investors are moody. They buy only when they want to do so. They are sometimes inconveniently reluctant. Corporate investors, if controlled, may be made to buy when the bankers need a market. It was natural that the investment bankers proceeded to get control of the great life insurance companies, as well as of the trust companies and the banks.

The field thus occupied is uncommonly rich. The life insurance companies are our leading institutions for savings. Their huge surplus and reserves, augmented daily, are always clamoring for investment. No panic or money shortage stops the inflow of new money from the perennial stream of premiums on existing policies and interest on existing investments. The three great companies—the New York Life, the Mutual of New York, and the Equitable—would have over $55,000,000 of *new* money to invest annually, even if they did not issue a single new policy. In 1904—just before the Armstrong investigation—these three companies had together $1,247,331,738.18 of assets. They had issued in that year $1,025,671,126 of new policies. The New York legislature placed in 1906 certain restrictions upon their growth; so that their new business since has averaged $547,384,212, or only fifty-three per cent. of what it was in 1904. But the aggregate assets of these companies increased in the last eight years to $1,817,052,260.36. At the time of the Armstrong investigation the average age of these three companies was fifty-six years. *The growth of assets in the last eight years was about half as large as the total growth in the preceding fifty-six years.* These three companies must invest annually about $70,000,000 of new money; and besides, many old investments expire or are changed and the proceeds must be reinvested. A large part of all life insurance surplus and reserves are invested in bonds. The aggregate bond investments of these three companies on January 1, 1913, was $1,019,153,268.93.

It was natural that the investment bankers should seek to control these never-failing reservoirs of capital. George W. Perkins was Vice-President of the New York Life, the largest of the companies. While remaining such he was made a partner in J. P. Morgan & Co., and in the four years preceding the Armstrong investigation, his firm sold the New York Life $38,804,918.51 in securities. The New York Life is a mutual company, supposed to be controlled by its policy-holders. But, as the Pujo Committee found "the so-called control of life insurance companies by policy-holders through mutualization is a farce" and "its only result is to keep in office a self-constituted, self-perpetuating management."

The Equitable Life Assurance Society is a stock company and is controlled by $100,000 of stock. The dividend on this stock is limited by law to seven per cent.; but in 1910 Mr. Morgan paid about $3,000,000 for $51,000, par value of this stock, or $5,882.35 a share. The dividend return on the stock investment is less than one-eighth of one per cent.; but the assets controlled amount now to over $500,000,000. And certain of these assets had an especial value for investment bankers;—namely, the large holdings of stock in banks and trust companies.

The Armstrong investigation disclosed the extent of financial power exerted through the insurance company holdings of bank and trust company stock. The Committee recommended legislation compelling the insurance companies to dispose of the stock within five years. A law to that effect was enacted, but the time was later extended. The companies then disposed of a part of their bank and trust company stocks; but, as the insurance companies were controlled by the investment bankers, these gentlemen sold the bank and trust company stocks to themselves.

Referring to such purchases from the Mutual Life, as well as from the Equitable, the Pujo Committee found:

> Here, then, were stocks of five important trust companies and one of our largest national banks in New York City that had been held by these two life insurance companies. Within five years all of these stocks, so far as distributed by the insurance companies, have found their way into the hands of the men who virtually controlled or were identified with the management of the insurance companies or of their close allies and associates, to that extent thus further entrenching them.

The banks and trust companies are depositaries, in the main, not of the people's savings, but of the business man's quick capital. Yet, since the investment banker acquired control of banks and trust companies, these institutions also have become, like the life companies, large purchasers of bonds and stocks. Many of our national banks have invested in this manner a large part of all their resources, including capital, surplus, and deposits. The bond investments of some banks exceed by far the aggregate of their capital and surplus, and nearly equal their loanable deposits.

Controlling Other People's Quick Capital

The goose that lays golden eggs has been considered a most valuable possession. But even more profitable is the privilege of taking the golden eggs laid by somebody else's goose. The investment bankers and their associates now enjoy that privilege. They control the people through the people's own money. If the bankers' power were commensurate only with their wealth, they would have relatively little influence on American business. Vast fortunes like those of the Astors are no doubt regrettable. They are inconsistent with democracy. They are unsocial. And they seem peculiarly unjust when they represent largely unearned increment. But the wealth of the Astors does not endanger political or industrial liberty. It is insignificant in amount as compared with the aggregate wealth of America, or even of New York City. It lacks significance largely because its owners have only the income from their own wealth. The Astor wealth is static.

operations of these bankers are so vast and numerous that even a very reasonable compensation for the service performed by the bankers, would, in the aggregate, produce for them incomes so large as to result in huge accumulations of capital. But the compensation taken by the bankers as commissions or profits is often far from reasonable. Occupying, as they so frequently do, the inconsistent position of being at the same time seller and buyer, the standard for so-called compensation actually applied, is not the "Rule of reason," but "All the traffic will bear." And this is true even where there is no sinister motive. The weakness of human nature prevents men from being good judges of their own deservings.

The syndicate formed by J. P. Morgan & Co. to underwrite the United States Steel Corporation took for its services securities which netted $62,500,000 in cash. Of this huge sum J. P. Morgan & Co. received, as syndicate managers, $12,500,000 in addition to the share which they were entitled to receive as syndicate members. This sum of $62,500,000 was only a part of the fees paid for the service of monopolizing the steel industry. In addition to the commissions taken specifically for organizing the United States Steel Corporation, large sums were paid for organizing the several companies of which it is composed. For instance, the National Tube Company was capitalized at $80,000,000 of stock; $40,000,000 of which was common stock. Half of this $40,000,000 was taken by J. P. Morgan & Co. and their associates for promotion services; and the $20,000,000 stock so taken became later exchangeable for $25,000,000 of Steel Common. Commissioner of Corporations Herbert Knox Smith found that:

> More than $150,000,000 of the stock of the Steel Corporation was issued directly or indirectly (through exchange) for mere promotion or underwriting services. In other words, nearly one-seventh of the total capital stock of the Steel Corporation appears to have been issued directly or indirectly to promoters' services.

The so-called fees and commissions taken by the bankers and associates upon the organization of the trusts have been exceptionally large. But even after the trusts are successfully launched the exactions of the bankers are often extortionate. The syndicate which underwrote, in 1901, the Steel Corporation's preferred stock conversion plan, advanced only $20,000,000 in cash and received an underwriting commission of $6,800,000.

The exaction of huge commissions is not confined to trusts and other industrial concerns. The Interborough Railway is a most prosperous corporation. It earned last year nearly 21 per cent. on its capital stock, and secured from New York City, in connection with the subway extension, a very favorable contract. But when it financed its $170,000,000 bond issue it was agreed that J. P. Morgan & Co. should receive three per cent., that is, $5,100,000, for merely forming this syndicate. More recently, the New York, New Haven & Hartford Railroad agreed to pay J. P. Morgan & Co. a commission of $1,680,000; that is, 2½ per cent., to form a syndicate to underwrite an issue at par of $67,000,000 20-year 6 per cent. convertible debentures. That means: The bankers bound themselves to take at 97½ any of these six per cent. convertible bonds which stockholders might be unwilling to buy at 100. When the contract was made the New Haven's then outstanding six per cent. convertible bonds were selling at 114. And the new issue, as soon as announced, was in such demand that the public offered and was for months willing to buy at 106 bonds which the Company were to pay J. P. Morgan & Co. $1,680,000 to be willing to take at par.

Why the Banks Became Investment Bankers

These large profits from promotions, underwritings, and security purchases led to a revolutionary change in the conduct of our leading banking institutions. It was obvious that control by the investment bankers of the deposits in banks and trust companies was an essential element in their securing these huge profits. And the bank officers naturally asked, "Why then should not the banks and trust companies share in so profitable a field? Why should not they themselves become investment bankers too, with all the new functions incident to 'Big Business'?" To do so would involve a departure from the legitimate sphere of the banking business, which is the making of temporary loans to business concerns. But the temptation was irresistible. The invasion of the investment banker into the banks' field of operation was followed by a counter invasion by the banks into the realm of the investment banker. Most prominent among the banks were the National City and the First National of New York. But theirs was not a hostile invasion. The contending forces met as allies, joined forces to control the business of the country, and to "divide the spoils." The alliance was cemented by voting trusts, by interlocking directories, and by joint ownerships. There resulted the fullest "cooperation"; and ever more railroads, public service corporations, and industrial concerns were brought into complete subjection.

Chapter II

How the Combiners Combine

Among the allies, two New York banks—the National City and the First National—stand preeminent. They constitute, with the Morgan firm, the inner group of the Money Trust. Each of the two banks, like J. P. Morgan & Co., has huge resources. Each of the two banks, like the firm of J. P. Morgan & Co., has been dominated by a genius in combination. In the National City it is James Stillman; in the First National, George F. Baker. Each of these gentlemen was formerly President, and is now Chairman of the Board of Directors. The resources of the National City Bank (including its Siamese-twin security company) are about $300,000,000; those of the First National Bank (including its Siamese-twin security company) are about $200,000,000. The resources of the Morgan firm have not been disclosed. But it appears that they have available for their operations, also, huge deposits from their subjects; deposits reported as $162,500,000.

The private fortunes of the chief actors in the combination have not been ascertained. But sporadic evidence indicates how great are the possibilities of accumulation when one has the use of "other people's money." Mr. Morgan's wealth became proverbial. Of Mr. Stillman's many investments, only one was specifically referred to, as he was in Europe during the investigation, and did not testify. But that one is significant. His 47,498 shares in the National City Bank are worth about $18,000,000. Mr. Jacob H. Schiff aptly described this as "a very nice investment."

Of Mr. Baker's investments we know more, as he testified on many subjects. His 20,000 shares in the First National Bank are worth at least $20,000,000. His stocks in six other New York banks and trust companies are together worth about $3,000,000. The scale of his investment in railroads may be inferred from his former holdings in the Central Railroad of New Jersey. He was its largest stockholder—so large that with a few friends he held a majority of the $27,436,800 par value of outstanding stock, which the Reading bought at $160 a share. He is a director in 28 other railroad companies; and presumably a stockholder in, at least, as many. The full extent of his fortune was not inquired into, for that was not an issue in the investigation. But it is not surprising that Mr. Baker saw little need of new laws. When asked: "You think everything is all right as it is in this world, do you not?"

He answered: "Pretty nearly."

Ramifications of Power

But wealth expressed in figures gives a wholly inadequate picture of the allies' power. Their wealth is dynamic. It is wielded by geniuses in combination. It finds its proper expression in means of control. To comprehend the power of the allies we must try to visualize the ramifications through which the forces operate.

Mr. Baker is a director in 22 corporations having, with their many subsidiaries, aggregate resources or capitalization of $7,272,000,000. But the direct and visible power of the First National Bank, which Mr. Baker dominates, extends further. The Pujo report shows that its directors (including Mr. Baker's son) are directors in at least 27 other corporations with resources of $4,270,000,000. That is, the First National is represented in 49 corporations, with aggregate resources or capitalization of $11,542,000,000.

It may help to an appreciation of the allies' power to name a few of the more prominent corporations in which, for instance, Mr. Baker's influence is exerted—visibly and directly—as voting trustee, executive committee man, or simple director.

1. *Banks, Trust, and Life Insurance Companies:* First National Bank of New York; National Bank of Commerce; Farmers' Loan and Trust Company; Mutual Life Insurance Company.

2. *Railroad Companies:* New York Central Lines; New Haven, Reading, Erie, Lackawanna, Lehigh Valley, Southern, Northern Pacific, Chicago, Burlington & Quincy.

3. *Public Service Corporations:* American Telephone & Telegraph Company, Adams Express Company.

4. *Industrial Corporations:* United States Steel Corporation, Pullman Company.

Mr. Stillman is a director in only 7 corporations, with aggregate assets of $2,476,000,000; but the directors in the National City Bank, which he dominates, are directors in at least 41 other corporations which, with their subsidiaries, have an aggregate capitalization or resources of $10,564,000,000. The members of the firm of J. P. Morgan & Co., the acknowledged leader of the allied forces, hold 72 directorships in 47 of the largest corporations of the country.

The Pujo Committee finds that the members of J. P. Morgan & Co. and the directors of their controlled trust companies and of the First National and the National City Bank together hold:

One hundred and eighteen directorships in 34 banks and trust companies having total resources of $2,679,000,000 and total deposits of $1,983,000,000.

Thirty directorships in 10 insurance companies having total assets of $2,293,000,000.

One hundred and five directorships in 32 transportation systems having a total capitalization of $11,784,000,000 and a total mileage (excluding express companies and steamship lines) of 150,200.

Sixty-three directorships in 24 producing and trading corporations having a total capitalization of $3,339,000,000.

Twenty-five directorships in 12 public-utility corporations having a total capitalization of $2,150,000,000.

In all, 341 directorships in 112 corporations having aggregate resources or capitalization of $22,245,000,000.

Twenty-two Billion Dollars

Twenty-two billion dollars is a large sum—so large that we have difficulty in grasping its significance. The mind realizes size only through comparisons. With what can we compare twenty-two billions of dollars? Twenty-two billions of dollars is more than three times the assessed value of all the property, real and personal, in all New England. It is nearly three times the assessed value of all the real estate in the City of New York. It is more than twice the assessed value of all the property in the thirteen Southern states. It is more than the assessed value of all the property in the twenty-two states, north and south, lying west of the Mississippi River.

But the huge sum of twenty-two billion dollars is not large enough to include all the corporations to which the "influence" of the three allies directly and visibly extends, for

First: There are 56 other corporations (not included in the Pujo schedule) each with capital or resources of over $5,000,000, and aggregating nearly $1,350,000,000, in which the Morgan allies are represented according to the directories of directors.

Second: The Pujo schedule does not include any corporation with resources of less than $5,000,000. But these financial giants have shown their humility by becoming directors in many such. For instance, members of J. P. Morgan & Co., and directors in the National City Bank and the First National Bank are also directors in 158 such corporations. Available publications disclose the capitalization of only 38 of these, but those 38 aggregate $78,669,375.

Third: The Pujo schedule includes only the corporations in which the Morgan associates actually appear by name as directors. It does not include those in which they are represented by dummies, or otherwise. For instance, the Morgan influence certainly extends to the Kansas City Terminal Railroad Company, for which they have marketed since 1910 (in connection with others) four issues aggregating $41,761,000. But no member of J. P. Morgan & Co., of the National City Bank, or of the First National Bank appears on the Kansas City Terminal directorate.

Fourth: The Pujo schedule does not include all the subsidiaries of the corporations scheduled. For instance, the capitalization of the New Haven System is given as $385,000,000. That sum represents the bond and stock capital of the New Haven *Railroad.* But the New Haven *System* comprises many controlled corporations whose capitalization is only to a slight extent included directly or indirectly in the New Haven Railroad balance sheet. The New Haven, like most large corporations, is a holding company also; and a holding company may control subsidiaries while owning but a small part of the latters' outstanding securities. Only the small part so held will be represented in the holding company's balance sheet. Thus, while the New Haven Railroad's capitalization is only $385,000,000—and that sum only appears in the Pujo schedule—the capitalization of the New Haven System, as shown by a chart submitted to the Committee, is over twice as great; namely, $849,000,000.

It is clear, therefore, that the $22,000,000,000, referred to by the Pujo Committee, understates the extent of concentration effected by the inner group of the Money Trust.

Cementing the Triple Alliance

Care was taken by these builders of imperial power that their structure should be enduring. It has been buttressed on every side by joint ownerships and mutual stockholdings, as well as by close personal relationships; for directorships are ephemeral and may end with a new election. Mr. Morgan and his partners acquired one-sixth of the stock of the First National Bank, and made a $6,000,000 investment in the stock of the National City Bank. Then J. P. Morgan & Co., the National City, and the First National (or their dominant officers—Mr. Stillman and Mr. Baker) acquired together, by stock purchases and voting trusts, control of the National Bank of Commerce, with its $190,000,000 of resources; of the Chase National, with $125,000,000; of the Guaranty Trust Company, with $232,000,000; of the Bankers' Trust Company, with $205,000,000; and of a number of smaller, but important, financial institutions. They became joint voting trustees in great railroad systems; and finally (as if the allies were united into a single concern) loyal and efficient service in the banks—like that rendered by Mr. Davison and Mr. Lamont in the First National—was rewarded by promotion to membership in the firm of J. P. Morgan & Co.

The Provincial Allies

Thus equipped and bound together, J. P. Morgan & Co., the National City, and the First National easily dominated America's financial center, New York; for certain other important bankers, to be hereafter mentioned, were held in restraint by "gentlemen's" agreements. The three allies dominated Philadelphia too; for the firm of Drexel & Co. is J. P. Morgan & Co. under another name. But there are two other important money centers in America, Boston and Chicago.

In Boston there are two large international banking houses—Lee, Higginson & Co., and Kidder, Peabody & Co.—both long established and rich; and each possessing an extensive, wealthy clientele of eager investors in bonds and stocks. Since 1907 each of these firms has purchased or underwritten (principally in conjunction with other bankers) about 100 different security issues of the greater interstate corporations, the issues of each banker amounting in the aggregate to over $1,000,000,000. Concentration of banking capital has proceeded even further in Boston than in New York. By successive consolidations the number of national banks has been reduced from 58 in 1898 to 19 in 1913. There are in Boston now also 23 trust companies.

The National Shawmut Bank, the First National Bank of Boston, and the Old Colony Trust Co., which these two Boston banking houses and their associates control, alone have aggregate resources of $288,386,294, constituting about one-half of the banking resources of the city. These great banking institutions, which are themselves the result of many consolidations, and the 21 other banks and trust companies, in which their directors are also directors, hold together 90 per cent. of the total banking resources of Boston. And linked to them by interlocking directorates are 9 other banks and trust companies whose aggregate resources are about 2½ per cent. of Boston's total. Thus of 42 banking institutions, 33, with aggregate resources of $560,516,239, holding about 92½ per cent. of the aggregate banking resources of Boston, are interlocked. But even the remaining 9 banks and trust companies, which together hold but 7½ per cent. of Boston banking resources, are not all independent of one another. Three are linked together; so that there appear to be only six banks in all

Boston that are free from interlocking directorate relations. They together represent but 5 per cent. of Boston's banking resources. And it may well be doubted whether all of even those 6 are entirely free from affiliation with the other groups.

Boston's banking concentration is not limited to the legal confines of the city. Around Boston proper are over thirty suburbs, which with it form what is popularly known as "Greater Boston." These suburban municipalities, and also other important cities like Worcester and Springfield, are, in many respects, within Boston's "sphere of influence." Boston's inner banking group has interlocked, not only 33 of the 42 banks of Boston proper, as above shown, but has linked with them, by interlocking directorships, at least 42 other banks and trust companies in 35 other municipalities.

Once Lee, Higginson & Co. and Kidder, Peabody & Co. were active competitors. They are so still in some small, or purely local matters; but both are devoted co-operators with the Morgan associates in larger and interstate transactions; and the alliance with these great Boston banking houses has been cemented by mutual stockholdings and co-directorships. Financial concentration seems to have found its highest expression in Boston.

Somewhat similar relations exist between the triple alliance and Chicago's great financial institutions—its First National Bank, the Illinois Trust and Savings Bank, and the Continental & Commercial National Bank— which together control resources of $561,000,000. And similar relations would doubtless be found to exist with the leading bankers of the other important financial centers of America, as to which the Pujo Committee was prevented by lack of time from making investigation.

The Auxiliaries

Such are the primary, such the secondary powers which comprise the Money Trust; but these are supplemented by forces of magnitude.

"Radiating from these principal groups," says the Pujo Committee, "and closely affiliated with them are smaller but important banking houses, such as Kissel, Kinnicut & Co., White, Weld & Co., and Harvey Fisk & Sons, who receive large and lucrative patronage from the dominating groups, and are used by the latter as jobbers or distributors of securities, the issuing of which they control, but which for reasons of their own they prefer not to have issued or distributed under their own names. Lee, Higginson & Co., besides being partners with the inner group, are also frequently utilized in this service because of their facilities as distributors of securities."

For instance, J. P. Morgan & Co. as fiscal agents of the New Haven Railroad had the right to market its securities and that of its subsidiaries. Among the numerous New Haven subsidiaries, is the New York, Westchester, and Boston—the road which cost $1,500,000 a mile to build, and which earned a *deficit* last year of nearly $1,500,000, besides failing to earn any return upon the New Haven's own stock and bond investment of $8,241,951. When the New Haven concluded to market $17,200,000 of these bonds, J. P. Morgan & Co., "for reasons of their own," "preferred not to have these bonds issued or distributed under their own name." The Morgan firm took the bonds at 92½ net; and the bonds were marketed by Kissel, Kinnicut & Co. and others at 96¼.

The Satellites

The alliance is still further supplemented, as the Pujo Committee shows:

Beyond these inner groups and sub-groups are banks and bankers throughout the country who co-operate with them in underwriting or guaranteeing the sale of securities offered to the public, and who also act as distributors of such securities. It was impossible to learn the identity of these corporations, owing to the unwillingness of the members of the inner group to disclose the names of their underwriters, but sufficient appears to justify the statement that there are at least hundreds of them and that they extend into many of the cities throughout this and foreign countries.

The patronage thus proceeding from the inner group and its sub-groups is of great value to these banks and bankers, who are thus tied by self-interest to the great issuing houses and may be regarded as a part of this vast financial organization. Such patronage yields no inconsiderable part of the income of these banks and bankers and without much risk on account of the facilities of the principal groups for placing issues of securities through their domination of great banks and trust companies and their other domestic affiliations and their foreign connections. The underwriting commissions on issues made by this inner group are usually easily earned and do not ordinarily involve the underwriters in the purchase of the underwritten securities. Their interest in the transaction is generally adjusted unless they choose to purchase part of the securities, by the payment to them of a commission. There are, however, occasions on which this is not the case. The underwriters are then required to take the securities. Bankers and brokers are so anxious to be permitted to participate in these transactions under the lead of the inner group that as a rule they join when invited to do so, regardless of their approval of the particular business, lest by refusing they should thereafter cease to be invited.

In other words, an invitation from these royal bankers is interpreted as a command. As a result, these great bankers frequently get huge commissions without themselves distributing any of the bonds, or ever having taken any actual risk.

In the case of the New York subway financing of $170,000,000 of bonds by Messrs. Morgan & Co. and their associates, Mr. Davison [as the Pujo Committee reports] estimated that there were from 100 to 125 such underwriters who were apparently glad to agree that Messrs. Morgan & Co., the First National Bank, and the National City Bank should receive 3 per cent.—equal to $5,100,000—for forming this syndicate, thus relieving themselves from all liability, whilst the underwriters assumed the risk of what the bonds would realize and of being required to take their share of the unsold portion.

The Protection of Pseudo-ethics

The organization of the Money Trust is intensive, the combination comprehensive; but one other element was recognized as necessary to render it stable, and to make its dynamic force irresistible. Despotism, be it financial or political, is vulnerable, unless it is believed to rest upon a moral sanction. The longing for freedom is ineradicable. It will express itself in protest against servitude and inaction, unless the striving for freedom be made to seem immoral. Long ago monarchs invented, as a preservative of absolutism, the fiction of "The divine right of kings." Bankers, imitating royalty, invented recently that precious rule of so-called "Ethics," by which it is declared unprofessional to come to the financial relief of any corporation which is already the prey of another "reputable" banker.

"The possibility of competition between these banking houses in the purchase of securities," says the Pujo Committee, "is further removed by the understanding between them and others, that one will not seek, by offering better terms, to take away from another, a customer which it has theretofore served, and by corollary of this, namely, that where given bankers have once satisfactorily united in bringing out an issue of a corporation, they shall also join in bringing out any subsequent issue of the same corporations. This is described as a principle of banking ethics."

The "Ethical" basis of the rule must be that the interests of the combined bankers are superior to the interests of the rest of the community. Their attitude reminds one of the "spheres of influence" with ample "hinterlands" by which rapacious nations are adjusting differences. Important banking concerns, too ambitious to be willing to take a subordinate position in the alliance, and too powerful to be suppressed, are accorded a financial "sphere of influence" upon the understanding that the rule of banking ethics will be faithfully observed. Most prominent among such lesser potentates are Kuhn, Loeb & Co., of New York, an international banking house of great wealth, with large clientele and connections. They are accorded an important "sphere of influence" in American railroading, including among other systems the Baltimore & Ohio, the Union Pacific, and the Southern Pacific. They and the Morgan group have with few exceptions preempted the banking business of the important railroads of the country. But even Kuhn, Loeb & Co. are not wholly independent. The Pujo Committee reports that they are "qualified allies of the inner group"; and through their "close relations with the National City Bank and the National Bank of Commerce and other financial institutions" have "many interests in common with the Morgan associates, conducting large joint-account operations with them."

The Evils Resultant

First: These banker-barons levy, through their excessive exactions, a heavy toll upon the whole community; upon owners of money for leave to invest it; upon railroads, public service, and industrial companies, for leave to use this money of other people; and, through these corporations, upon consumers.

"The charge of capital," says the Pujo Committee, "which of course enters universally into the price of commodities and of service, is thus in effect determined by agreement amongst those supplying it and not under the check of competition. If there be any virtue in the principle of competition, certainly any plan or arrangement which prevents its operation in the performance of so fundamental a commercial function as the supplying of capital is peculiarly injurious."

Second: More serious, however, is the effect of the Money Trust in directly suppressing competition. That suppression enables the monopolist to extort excessive profits; but monopoly increases the burden of the consumer even more in other ways. Monopoly arrests development; and through arresting development, prevents that lessening of the cost of production and of distribution which would otherwise take place.

Can full competition exist among the anthracite coal railroads when the Morgan associates are potent in all of them? And with like conditions prevailing, what competition is to be expected between the Northern Pacific and the Great Northern, the Southern, the Louisville and Nashville, and the Atlantic Coast Line; or between the Westinghouse Manufacturing Company and the General Electric Company? As the Pujo Committee finds:

Such affiliations tend as a cover and conduit for secret arrangements and understandings in restriction of competition through the agency of the banking house thus situated.

And under existing conditions of combination, relief through other banking houses is precluded.

It can hardly be expected that the banks, trust companies, and other institutions that are thus seeking participation from this inner group would be likely to engage in business of a character that would be displeasing to the latter or would interfere with their plans or prestige. And so the protection that can be afforded by the members of the inner group constitutes the safest refuge of our great industrial combinations against future competition. The powerful grip of these gentlemen is upon the throttle that controls the wheels of credit, and upon their signal those wheels will turn or stop.

Third: But far more serious even than the suppression of competition is the suppression of industrial liberty, indeed of manhood itself, which this overweening financial power entails. The intimidation which it effects extends far beyond "the banks, trust companies, and other institutions seeking participation from this inner group in their lucrative underwritings"; and far beyond those interested in the great corporations directly dependent upon the inner group. Its blighting and benumbing effect extends as well to the small and seemingly independent business man, to the vast army of professional men and others directly dependent upon "Big Business," and to many another; for

1. Nearly every enterprising business man needs bank credit. The granting of credit involves the exercise of judgment of the bank officials; and however honestly the bank officials may wish to exercise their discretion, experience shows that their judgment is warped by the existence of the all-pervading power of the Money Trust. He who openly opposes the great interests will often be found to lack that quality of "safe and sane"-ness which is the basis of financial credit.

2. Nearly every enterprising business man and a large part of our professional men have something to sell to, or must buy something from, the great corporations to which the control or influence of the money lords extends directly, or from or to affiliated interests. Sometimes it is merchandise; sometimes it is service; sometimes they have nothing either to buy or to sell, but desire political or social advancement. Sometimes they want merely peace. Experience shows that "it is not healthy to buck against a locomotive," and "Business is business."

Here and there you will find a hero—red-blooded, and courageous—loving manhood more than wealth, place or security—who dared to fight for independence and won. Here and there you may find the martyr, who resisted in silence and suffered with resignation. But America, which seeks "the greatest good of the greatest number," cannot be content with conditions that fit only the hero, the martyr, or the slave.

Chapter III

Interlocking Directorates

The practice of interlocking directorates is the root of many evils. It offends laws human and divine. Applied to rival corporations, it tends to the suppression of competition and to violation of the Sherman law. Applied to corporations which deal with each other, it tends to disloyalty and to violation of the fundamental law that no man can serve two masters. In either event it tends to inefficiency; for it removes incentive and destroys soundness of judgment. It is undemocratic, for it rejects the platform: "A fair field and no favors"—substituting the pull of privilege for the push of manhood. It is the most potent instrument of the Money Trust. Break the control so exercised by the investment bankers over railroads, public-service and industrial corporations, over banks, life insurance and trust companies, and a long step will have been taken toward attainment of the New Freedom.

The term "interlocking directorates" is here used in a broad sense as including all intertwined conflicting interests, whatever the form, and by whatever device effected. The objection extends alike to contracts of a corporation whether with one of its directors individually, or with a firm of which he is a member, or with another corporation in which he is interested as an officer or director or stockholder. The objection extends likewise to men holding the inconsistent position of director in two potentially competing corporations, even if those corporations do not actually deal with each other.

The Endless Chain

A single example will illustrate the vicious circle of control—the endless chain—through which our financial oligarchy now operates:

J. P. Morgan (or a partner), a director of the New York, New Haven & Hartford Railroad, causes that company to sell to J. P. Morgan & Co. an issue of bonds. J. P. Morgan & Co. borrow the money with which to pay for the bonds from the Guaranty Trust Company, of which Mr. Morgan (or a partner) is a director. J. P. Morgan & Co. sell the bonds to the Penn Mutual Life Insurance Company, of which Mr. Morgan (or a partner) is a director. The New Haven spends the proceeds of the bonds in purchasing steel rails from the United States Steel Corporation, of which Mr. Morgan (or a partner) is a director. The United States Steel Corporation spends the proceeds of the rails in purchasing electrical supplies from the General Electric Company, of which Mr. Morgan (or a partner) is a director. The General Electric sells supplies to the Western Union Telegraph Company, a subsidiary of the American Telephone and Telegraph Company; and in both Mr. Morgan (or a partner) is a director. The Telegraph Company has an exclusive wire contract with the Reading, of which Mr. Morgan (or a partner) is a director. The Reading buys its passenger cars from the Pullman Company, of which Mr. Morgan (or a partner) is a director. The Pullman Company buys (for local use) locomotives from the Baldwin Locomotive Company, of which Mr. Morgan (or a partner) is a director. The Reading, the General Electric, the Steel Corporation and the New Haven, like the Pullman, buy locomotives from the Baldwin Company. The Steel Corporation, the Telephone Company, the New Haven, the Reading, the Pullman, and the Baldwin Companies, like the Western Union, buy electrical supplies from the General Electric. The Baldwin, the Pullman, the Reading, the Telephone, the Telegraph, and the General Electric companies, like the New Haven, buy steel products from the Steel Corporation. Each and every one of the companies last named markets its securities through J. P. Morgan & Co.; each deposits its funds with J. P. Morgan & Co.; and with these funds of each, the firm enters upon further operations.

This specific illustration is in part supposititious; but it represents truthfully the operation of interlocking directorates. Only it must be multiplied many times and with many permutations to represent fully the extent to which the interests of a few men are intertwined. Instead of taking the New Haven as the railroad starting point in our example, the New York Central, the Santa Fe, the Southern, the Lehigh Valley, the Chicago and Great Western, the Erie, or the Père Marquette might have been selected; instead of the Guaranty Trust Company as the banking reservoir, any one of a dozen other important banks or trust companies; instead of the Penn Mutual as purchaser of the bonds, other insurance companies; instead of the General Electric, its qualified competitor, the Westinghouse

Electric and Manufacturing Company. The chain is indeed endless; for each controlled corporation is entwined with many others. As the nexus of "Big Business" the Steel Corporation stands, of course, preeminent. The Stanley Committee* showed that the few men who control the Steel Corporation, itself an owner of important railroads, are directors also in twenty-nine other railroad systems, with 126,000 miles of line (more than half the railroad mileage of the United States), and in important steamship companies. Through all these alliances and the huge traffic it controls, the Steel Corporation's influence pervades railroad and steamship companies—not as carriers only—but as the largest customers for steel. And its influence with users of steel extends much further. These same few men are also directors in twelve steel-using street railway systems, including some of the largest in the world. They are directors in forty machinery and similar steel-using manufacturing companies; in many gas, oil, and water companies, extensive users of iron products; and in the great wire-using telephone and telegraph companies. The aggregate assets of these different corporations—through which these few men exert their influence over the business of the United States—exceeds sixteen billion dollars.

Obviously, interlocking directorates, and all that term implies, must be effectually prohibited before the freedom of American business can be regained. The prohibition will not be an innovation. It will merely give full legal sanction to the fundamental law of morals and of human nature: that "No man can serve two masters." The surprising fact is that a principle of equity so firmly rooted should have been departed from at all in dealing with corporations. For no rule of law has, in other connections, been more rigorously applied, than that which prohibits a trustee from occupying inconsistent positions, from dealing with himself, or from using his fiduciary position for personal profit. And a director of a corporation is as obviously a trustee as persons holding similar positions in an unincorporated association, or in a private trust estate, who are called specifically by that name. The Courts have recognized this fully.

Thus, the Court of Appeals of New York declared in an important case:

> While not technically trustees, for the title of the corporate property was in the corporation itself, they were charged with the duties and subject to the liabilities of trustees. Clothed with the power of controlling the property and managing the affairs of the corporation without let or hindrance, as to third persons, they were its agents; but as to the

---

* Congressman *Augustus O. Stanley* of Kentucky headed a congressional investigation into the activities of the U.S. Steel Corporation in early 1912.

corporation itself equity holds them liable as trustees. While courts of law generally treat the directors as agents, courts of equity treat them as trustees, and hold them to a strict account for any breach of the trust relation. For all practical purposes they are trustees, when called upon in equity to account for their official conduct.

Nullifying the Law

But this wholesome rule of business, so clearly laid down, was practically nullified by courts in creating two unfortunate limitations, as concessions doubtless to the supposed needs of commerce.

First: Courts held valid contracts between a corporation and a director, or between two corporations with a common director, where it was shown that in making the contract, the corporation was represented by independent directors and that the vote of the interested director was unnecessary to carry the motion and his presence was not needed to constitute a quorum.

Second: Courts held that even where a common director participated actively in the making of a contract between two corporations, the contract was not absolutely void, but voidable only at the election of the corporation.

The first limitation ignored the rule of law that a beneficiary is entitled to disinterested advice from *all* his trustees, and not merely from some; and that a trustee may violate his trust by inaction as well as by action. It ignored, also, the laws of human nature, in assuming that the influence of a director is confined to the act of voting. Every one knows that the most effective work is done before any vote is taken, subtly, and without provable participation. Every one should know that the denial of minority representation on boards of directors has resulted in the domination of most corporations by one or two men; and in practically banishing all criticism of the dominant power. And even where the board is not so dominated, there is too often that "harmonious cooperation" among directors which secures for each, in his own line, a due share of the corporation's favors.

The second limitation—by which contracts, in the making of which the interested director participates actively, are held *merely voidable* instead of absolutely void—ignores the teachings of experience. To hold such contracts merely voidable has resulted practically in declaring them valid. It is the directors who control corporate action; and there is little reason to expect that any contract, entered into by a board with a fellow director, however unfair, would be subsequently avoided. Appeals from Philip drunk to Philip sober are not of frequent occurrence, nor very fruitful. But here we lack even an appealing party. Directors and the dominant stockholders would, of course, not appeal; and the minority stockholders have rarely the knowledge of facts which is essential to an effective appeal, whether it be made to the directors, to the whole body of stockholders, or to the courts. Besides, the financial burden and the risks incident to any attempt of individual stockholders to interfere with an existing management is ordinarily prohibitive. Proceedings to avoid contracts with directors are, therefore, seldom brought, except after a radical change in the membership of the board. And radical changes in a board's membership are rare. Indeed the Pujo Committee reports:

> None of the witnesses (the leading American bankers testified) was able to name an instance in the history of the country in which the stockholders had succeeded in overthrowing an existing management in any large corporation. Nor does it appear that stockholders have ever even succeeded in so far as to secure the investigation of an existing management of a corporation to ascertain whether it has been well or honestly managed.

Mr. Max Pam* proposed in the April, 1913, *Harvard Law Review,* that the government come to the aid of minority stockholders. He urged that the president of every corporation be required to report annually to the stockholders, and to state and federal officials every contract made by the company in which any director is interested; that the Attorney-General of the United States or the State investigate the same and take proper proceedings to set all such contracts aside and recover any damages suffered; or without disaffirming the contracts to recover from the interested directors the profits derived therefrom. And to this end also, that State and National Bank Examiners, State Superintendents of Insurance, and the Interstate Commerce Commission be directed to examine the records of every bank, trust company, insurance company, railroad company, and every other corporation engaged in interstate commerce. Mr. Pam's views concerning interlocking directorates are entitled to careful study. As counsel prominently identified with the organization of trusts, he had for years full opportunity of weighing the advantages and disadvantages of "Big Business." His conviction that the practice of interlocking directorates is a menace to the public and demands drastic legislation, is significant. And much can be said in support of the specific measure

---

* *Max Pam* was a public-spirited Chicago corporation lawyer whose work attacking interlocking directorates Brandeis used in writing *Other People's Money.*

which he proposes. But to be effective, the remedy must be fundamental and comprehensive.

The Essentials of Protection

Protection to minority stockholders demands that corporations be prohibited absolutely from making contracts in which a director has a private interest, and that all such contracts be declared not voidable merely, but absolutely void.

In the case of railroads and public-service corporations (in contradistinction to private industrial companies), such prohibition is demanded, also, in the interests of the general public. For interlocking interests breed inefficiency and disloyalty; and the public pays, in higher rates or in poor service, a large part of the penalty for graft and inefficiency. Indeed, whether rates are adequate or excessive cannot be determined until it is known whether the gross earnings of the corporation are properly expended. For when a company's important contracts are made through directors who are interested on both sides, the common presumption that money spent has been properly spent does not prevail. And this is particularly true in railroading, where the company so often lacks effective competition in its own field.

But the compelling reason for prohibiting interlocking directorates is neither the protection of stockholders, nor the protection of the public from the incidents of inefficiency and graft. Conclusive evidence (if obtainable) that the practice of interlocking directorates benefited all stockholders and was the most efficient form of organization, would not remove the objections. For even more important than efficiency are industrial and political liberty; and these are imperiled by the Money Trust. *Interlocking directorates must be prohibited, because it is impossible to break the Money Trust without putting an end to the practice in the larger corporations.*

Banks as Public-Service Corporations

The practice of interlocking directorates is peculiarly objectionable when applied to banks, because of the nature and functions of those institutions. Bank deposits are an important part of our currency system. They are almost as essential a factor in commerce as our railways. Receiving deposits and making loans therefrom should be treated by the law not as a private business, but as one of the public services. And recognizing it to be such, the law already regulates it in many ways. The function of a bank is to receive and to loan money. It has no more right than a common carrier to use its powers specifically to build up or to destroy other businesses. The granting or withholding of a loan should be determined, so far as concerns the borrower, solely by the interest rate and the risk involved; and not by favoritism or other considerations foreign to the banking function. Men may safely be allowed to grant or to deny loans of their *own* money to whomsoever they see fit, whatsoever their motive may be. But bank resources are, in the main, not owned by the stockholders nor by the directors. Nearly three-fourths of the aggregate resources of the thirty-four banking institutions in which the Morgan associates hold a predominant influence are represented by deposits. The dependence of commerce and industry upon bank deposits, as the common reservoir of quick capital is so complete, that deposit banking should be recognized as one of the businesses "affected with a public interest." And the general rule which forbids public-service corporations from making unjust discriminations or giving undue preference should be applied to the operations of such banks.

Senator Owen,* Chairman of the Committee on Banking and Currency, said recently:

My own judgment is that a bank is a public-utility institution and cannot be treated as a private affair, for the simple reason that the public is invited, under the safeguards of the government, to deposit its money with the bank, and the public has a right to have its interests safeguarded through organized authorities. The logic of this is beyond escape. All banks in the United States, public and private, should be treated as public-utility institutions, where they receive public deposits.

The directors and officers of banking institutions must, of course, be entrusted with wide discretion in the granting or denying of loans. But that discretion should be exercised, not only honestly as it affects stockholders, but also impartially as it affects the public. Mere honesty to the stockholders demands that the interests to be considered by the directors be the interests of all the stockholders; not the profit of the part of them who happen to be its directors. But the general welfare demands of the director, as trustee for the public, performance of a stricter duty. The fact that the granting of loans involves a delicate exercise of discretion makes it difficult to determine whether the rule of equality of treatment, which every public-service corporation owes, has been performed. But that difficulty merely emphasizes the importance of making absolute the rule that banks of deposit shall not make any loan nor engage in any transaction in which a director has a private interest. And we should bear this in mind:

*Robert L. Owen served as one of Oklahoma's senators from the time the state entered the Union in 1907 until his retirement in 1925.

If privately-owned banks fail in the public duty to afford borrowers equality of opportunity, there will arise a demand for government-owned banks, which will become irresistible.

The statement of Mr. Justice Holmes of the Supreme Court of the United States, in the Oklahoma Bank case,* is significant:

> We cannot say that the public interests to which we have adverted, and others, are not sufficient to warrant the State in taking the whole business of banking under its control. On the contrary we are of opinion that it may go on from regulation to prohibition except upon such conditions as it may prescribe.

Official Precedents

Nor would the requirement that banks shall make no loan in which a director has a private interest impose undue hardships or restrictions upon bank directors. It might make a bank director dispose of some of his investments and refrain from making others; but it often happens that the holding of one office precludes a man from holding another, or compels him to dispose of certain financial interests.

A judge is disqualified from sitting in any case in which he has even the smallest financial interest; and most judges, in order to be free to act in any matters arising in their court, proceed, upon taking office, to dispose of all investments which could conceivably bias their judgment in any matter that might come before them. An Interstate Commerce Commissioner** is prohibited from owning any bonds or stocks in any corporation subject to the jurisdiction of the Commission. It is a serious criminal offense for any executive officer of the federal government to transact government business with any corporation in the pecuniary profits of which he is directly or indirectly interested.

And the directors of our great banking institutions, as the ultimate judges of bank credit, exercise today a function no less important to the country's welfare than that of the judges of our courts, the interstate commerce commissioners, and departmental heads.

Scope of the Prohibition

In the proposals for legislation on this subject, four important questions are presented:

---

* In *Noble State Bank v. Haskell*, 219 U.S. 104 (1911), the Supreme Court had upheld Oklahoma's authority to compel banks to contribute to a state-run depositors' insurance fund.

** Congress had created the *Interstate Commerce Commission* in 1887 to oversee the operations of railroads and other interstate utilities such as telephones and telegraphs. Gradually the power of the Commission was expanded to include rate-setting authority.

1. Shall the principle of prohibiting interlocking directorates in potentially competing corporations be applied to state banking institutions, as well as the national banks?
2. Shall it be applied to all kinds of corporations or only to banking institutions?
3. Shall the principle of prohibiting corporations from entering into transactions in which the management has a private interest be applied to both directors and officers or be confined in its application to officers only?
4. Shall the principle be applied so as to prohibit transactions with another corporation in which one of its directors is interested merely as a stockholder?

Chapter IV

Serve One Master Only

The Pujo Committee has presented the facts concerning the Money Trust so clearly that the conclusions appear inevitable. Their diagnosis discloses intense financial concentration and the means by which it is effected. Combination—the intertwining of interests—is shown to be the all-pervading vice of the present system. With a view to freeing industry, the Committee recommends the enactment of twenty-one specific remedial provisions. Most of these measures are wisely framed to meet some abuse disclosed by the evidence; and if all of these were adopted the Pujo legislation would undoubtedly alleviate present suffering and aid in arresting the disease. But many of the remedies proposed are "local" ones; and a cure is not possible, without treatment which is fundamental. Indeed, a major operation is necessary. This the Committee has hesitated to advise; although the fundamental treatment required is simple: "Serve one Master only."

The evils incident to interlocking directorates are, of course, fully recognized; but the prohibitions proposed in that respect are restricted to a very narrow sphere.

First: The Committee recognizes that potentially competing corporations should not have a common director;—but it restricts this prohibition to directors of national banks, saying:

> No officer or director of a national bank shall be an officer or director of any other bank or of any trust company or other financial or other corporation or institution, whether organized under state or federal law,

that is authorized to receive money on deposit or that is engaged in the business of loaning money on collateral or in buying and selling securities except as in this section provided; and no person shall be an officer or director of any national bank who is a private banker or a member of a firm or partnership of bankers that is engaged in the business of receiving deposits: Provided, That such bank, trust company, financial institution, banker, or firm of bankers is located at or engaged in business at or in the same city, town, or village as that in which such national bank is located or engaged in business: Provided further, That a director of a national bank or a partner of such director may be an officer or director of not more than one trust company organized by the laws of the state in which such national bank is engaged in business and doing business at the same place.

Second: The Committee recognizes that a corporation should not make a contract in which one of the management has a private interest; but it restricts this prohibition (1) to national banks, and (2) to the officers, saying:

No national bank shall lend or advance money or credit or purchase or discount any promissory note, draft, bill of exchange or other evidence of debt bearing the signature or indorsement of any of its officers or of any partnership of which such officer is a member, directly or indirectly, or of any corporation in which such officer owns or has a beneficial interest of upward of ten per centum of the capital stock, or lend or advance money or credit to, for, or on behalf of any such officer or of any such partnership or corporation, or purchase any security from any such officer or of or from any partnership or corporation of which such officer is a member or in which he is financially interested, as herein specified, or of any corporation of which any of its officers is an officer at the time of such transaction.

Prohibitions of intertwining relations so restricted, however supplemented by other provisions, will not end financial concentration. The Money Trust snake will, at most, be scotched, not killed. The prohibition of a common director in potentially competing corporations should apply to state banks and trust companies, as well as to national banks; and it should apply to railroad and industrial corporations as fully as to banking institutions. The prohibition of corporate contracts in which one of the management has a private interest should apply to directors, as well as to officers, and to state banks and trust companies and to other classes of corporations, as well as to national banks. And, as will be hereafter shown, such broad legislation is within the power of Congress.

Let us examine this further:

The Prohibition of Common Directors
in Potentially Competing Corporations

1. *National Banks.* The objection to common directors, as applied to banking institutions, is clearly shown by the Pujo Committee.

As the first and foremost step in applying a remedy, and also for reasons that seem to us conclusive, independently of that consideration, we recommend that interlocking directorates in potentially competing financial institutions be abolished and prohibited as far as lies in the power of Congress to bring about that result. . . . When we find, as in a number of instances, the same man a director in half a dozen or more banks and trust companies all located in the same section of the same city, doing the same class of business and with a like set of associates similarly situated, all belonging to the same group and representing the same class of interests, all further pretense of competition is useless. . . . If banks serving the same field are to be permitted to have common directors, genuine competition will be rendered impossible. Besides, this practice gives to such common directors the unfair advantage of knowing the affairs of borrowers in various banks, and thus affords endless opportunities for oppression.

This recommendation is in accordance with the legislation or practice of other countries. The Bank of England, the Bank of France, the National Bank of Belgium, and the leading banks of Scotland all exclude from their boards persons who are directors in other banks. By law, in Russia no person is allowed to be on the board of management of more than one bank.

The Committee's recommendation is also in harmony with laws enacted by the Commonwealth of Massachusetts more than a generation ago designed to curb financial concentration through the savings banks. Of the great wealth of Massachusetts a large part is represented by deposits in its savings banks. These deposits are distributed among 194 different banks, located in 131 different cities and towns. These 194 banks are separate and distinct; not only in form, but in fact. In order that the banks may not be controlled by a few financiers, the Massachusetts law provides that no executive officer or trustee (director) of any savings bank can hold any office in any other savings bank. That statute was passed in 1876. A few years ago it was supplemented by providing that none of the executive officers of a savings bank could hold a similar office in any national bank. Massachusetts attempted thus to curb the power of the individual financier; and no disadvantages are discernible. When that Act was passed the aggregate deposits in its savings banks were $243,340,642; the number of deposit accounts 739,289; the average deposit to each person of the population $144. On November 1, 1912, the aggregate deposits were $838,635,097.85; the number of deposit accounts 2,200,917; the average deposit to each account $381.04. Massachusetts has shown that curbing the power of the few, at least in this respect, is entirely consistent with efficiency and with the prosperity of the whole people.

2. *State Banks and Trust Companies.* The reason for prohibiting common directors in banking institutions applies equally to national banks and to state banks including those trust companies which are essentially banks. In New York City there are 37 trust companies of which only 15 are members of the clearing house; but those 15 had on November 2, 1912, aggregate resources of $827,875,653. Indeed the Bankers' Trust Company with resources of $205,000,000, and the Guaranty Trust Company, with resources of $232,000,000, are among the most useful tools of the Money Trust. No bank in the country has larger deposits than the latter; and only one bank larger deposits than the former. If common directorships were permitted in state banks or such trust companies, the charters of leading national banks would doubtless soon be surrendered; and the institutions would elude federal control by re-incorporating under state laws.

The Pujo Committee has failed to apply the prohibition of common directorships in potentially competing banking institutions rigorously even to national banks. It permits the same man to be a director in one national bank and one trust company doing business in the same place. The proposed concession opens the door to grave dangers. In the first place the provision would permit the interlocking of any national bank not with one trust company only, but with as many trust companies as the bank has directors. For while under the Pujo bill no one can be a national bank director who is director in more than one such trust company, there is nothing to prevent each of the directors of a bank from becoming a director in a different trust company. The National Bank of Commerce of New York has a board of 38 directors. There are 37 trust companies in the City of New York. Thirty-seven of the 38 directors might each become a director of a different New York trust company: and thus 37 trust companies would be interlocked with the National Bank of Commerce, unless the other recommendation of the Pujo Committee limiting the number of directors to 13 were also adopted.

But even if the bill were amended so as to limit the possible interlocking of a bank to a single trust company, the wisdom of the concession would still be doubtful. It is true, as the Pujo Committee states, that "the business that may be transacted by" a trust company is of "a different character" from that properly transacted by a national bank. But the business actually conducted by a trust company is, at least in the East, quite similar; and the two classes of banking institutions have these vital elements in common: each is a bank of deposit, and each makes loans from its deposits. A private banker may also transact some business of a character different from that properly conducted by a bank; but by the terms of the Committee's bill a private banker engaged in the business of receiving deposits would be prevented from being a director of a national bank; and the reasons underlying that prohibition apply equally to trust companies and to private bankers.

3. *Other Corporations.* The interlocking of banking institutions is only one of the factors which have developed the Money Trust. The interlocking of other corporations has been an equally important element. And the prohibition of interlocking directorates should be extended to potentially competing corporations whatever the class; to life insurance companies, railroads and industrial companies, as well as banking institutions. The Pujo Committee has shown that Mr. George F. Baker is a common director in the six railroads which haul 80 per cent. of all anthracite marketed and own 88 per cent. of all anthracite deposits. The Morgan associates are the nexus between such supposedly competing railroads as the Northern Pacific and the Great Northern; the Southern, the Louisville & Nashville and the Atlantic Coast Line, and between partially competing industrials like the Westinghouse Electric and Manufacturing Company and the General Electric. The nexus between all the large potentially competing corporations must be severed, if the Money Trust is to be broken.

Prohibiting Corporate Contracts in Which the Management Has a Private Interest

The principle of prohibiting corporate contracts in which the management has a private interest is applied, in the Pujo Committee's recommendations, only to national banks, and in them only to officers. All other corporations are to be permitted to continue the practice; and even in national banks the directors are to be free to have a conflicting private interest, except that they must not accept compensation for promoting a loan of bank funds nor participate in syndicates, promotions, or underwriting of securities in which their banks may be interested as underwriters or owners or lenders thereon: that all loans or other transactions in which a director is interested shall be made in his own name; and shall be authorized only after ample notice to co-directors; and that the facts shall be spread upon the records of the corporation.

The Money Trust would not be disturbed by a prohibition limited to officers. Under a law of that character, financial control would continue to be exercised by the few without substantial impairment; but the power would be exerted through a somewhat different channel. Bank officers are appointees of the directors; and ordinarily their obedient servants. Individuals who, as bank officers, are now important factors in the financial concentration, would doubtless resign as officers and become merely directors. The loss of official salaries involved could be easily compensated. No member of the firm of J. P. Morgan & Co. is an officer in any one of the thirteen banking institutions with aggregate resources of $1,283,000,000, through which as directors they carry on their vast operations. A prohibition limited to officers would not affect the Morgan operations with these banking institutions. If there were minority representation on bank boards (which the Pujo Committee wisely advocates), such a provision might afford some protection to stockholders through the vigilance of the minority directors preventing the dominant directors using their power to the injury of the minority stockholders. But even then, the provision would not safeguard the public; and the primary purpose of Money Trust legislation is not to prevent directors from injuring stockholders; but to prevent their injuring the public through the intertwined control of the banks. No prohibition limited to officers will materially change this condition.

The prohibition of interlocking directorates, even if applied only to all banks and trust companies, would practically compel the Morgan representatives to resign from the directorates of the thirteen banking institutions with which they are connected, or from the directorates of all the railroads, express, steamship, public utility, manufacturing, and other corporations which do business with those banks and trust companies. Whether they resigned from the one or the other class of corporations, the endless chain would be broken into many pieces. And whether they retired or not, the Morgan power would obviously be greatly lessened: for if they did not retire, their field of operations would be greatly narrowed.

Apply the Private Interest Prohibition to All Kinds of Corporations

The creation of the Money Trust is due quite as much to the encroachment of the investment banker upon railroads, public service, industrial, and life-insurance companies, as to his control of banks and trust companies.

Before the Money Trust can be broken, all these relations must be severed. And they cannot be severed unless corporations of each of these several classes are prevented from dealing with their own directors and with corporations in which those directors are interested. For instance: The most potent single source of J. P. Morgan & Co.'s power is the $162,500,000 deposits, including those of 78 interstate railroad, public-service, and industrial corporations, which the Morgan firm is free to use as it sees fit. The proposed prohibition, even if applied to all banking institutions, would not affect directly this great source of Morgan power. If, however, the prohibition is made to include railroad, public-service, and industrial corporations, as well as banking institutions, members of J. P. Morgan & Co. will quickly retire from substantially all boards of directors.

Apply the Private Interest Prohibition to Stockholding Interests

The prohibition against one corporation entering into transactions with another corporation in which one of its directors is also interested, should apply even if his interest in the second corporation is merely that of stockholder. A conflict of interests in a director may be just as serious where he is a stockholder only in the second corporation, as if he were also a director.

One of the annoying petty monopolies, concerning which evidence was taken by the Pujo Committee, is the exclusive privilege granted to the American Bank Note Company by the New York Stock Exchange. A recent $60,000,000 issue of New York City bonds was denied listing on the Exchange, because the city refused to submit to an exaction of $55,800 by the American Company for engraving the bonds, when the New York Bank Note Company would do the work equally well for $44,500. As tending to explain this extraordinary monopoly, it was shown that men prominent in the financial world were stockholders in the American Company. Among the largest stockholders was Mr. Morgan, with 6,000 shares. No member of the Morgan firm was a director of the American Company; but there was sufficient influence exerted somehow to give the American Company the stock exchange monopoly.

The Pujo Committee, while failing to recommend that transactions in which a director has a private interest be prohibited, recognizes that a stockholder's interest of more than a certain size may be as potent an instrument of influence as a direct personal interest; for it recommends that:

Borrowings, directly or indirectly by . . . any corporation of the stock of which he (a bank director) holds upwards of 10 per cent. from the bank of which he is such director, should only be permitted, on condition that notice shall have been given to his co-directors and that a full statement of the transaction shall be entered upon the minutes of the meeting at which such loan was authorized.

As shown above, the particular provision for notice affords no protection to the public; but if it did, its application ought to be extended to lesser stock-holdings. Indeed it is difficult to fix a limit so low that financial interest will not influence action. Certainly a stockholding interest of a single director, much smaller than 10 per cent., might be most effective in inducing favors. Mr. Morgan's stockholdings in the American Bank Note Company were only three per cent. The $6,000,000 investment of J. P. Morgan & Co. in the National City Bank represented only 6 per cent. of the bank's stock; and would undoubtedly have been effective, even if it had not been supplemented by the election of his son to the board of directors.

Special Disqualifications

The Stanley Committee, after investigation of the Steel Trust, concluded that the evils of interlocking directorates were so serious that representatives of certain industries which are largely dependent upon railroads should be absolutely prohibited from serving as railroad directors, officers or employees. It, therefore, proposed to disqualify as railroad director, officer or employee any person engaged in the business of manufacturing or selling railroad cars or locomotives, railroad rail or structural steel, or in mining and selling coal. The drastic Stanley bill, shows how great is the desire to do away with present abuses and to lessen the power of the Money Trust.

Directors, officers, and employees of banking institutions should, by a similar provision, be disqualified from acting as directors, officers, or employees of life-insurance companies. The Armstrong investigation showed that life-insurance companies were in 1905 the most potent factor in financial concentration. Their power was exercised largely through the banks and trust companies which they controlled by stock ownership and their huge deposits. The Armstrong legislation directed life-insurance companies to sell their stocks. The Mutual Life and the Equitable did so in part. But the Morgan associates bought the stocks. And now, instead of the life-insurance companies controlling the banks and trust companies, the latter and the bankers control the life-insurance companies.

How the Prohibition
May Be Limited

The Money Trust cannot be destroyed unless all *classes* of corporations are included in the prohibition of interlocking directors and of transactions by corporations in which the management has a private interest. But it does not follow that the prohibition must apply to *every* corporation of each class. Certain exceptions are entirely consistent with merely protecting the public against the Money Trust; although protection of minority stockholders and business ethics demand that the rule prohibiting a corporation from making contracts in which a director has a private financial interest should be universal in its application. The number of corporations in the United States Dec. 31, 1912, was 305,336. Of these only 1610 have a capital of more than $5,000,000. Few corporations (other than banks) with a capital of less than $5,000,000 could appreciably affect general credit conditions either through their own operations or their affiliations. Corporations (other than banks) with capital resources of less than $5,000,000 might, therefore, be excluded from the scope of the statute for the present. The prohibition could also be limited so as not to apply to any industrial concern, regardless of the amount of capital and resources, doing only an intrastate business; as practically all large industrial corporations are engaged in interstate commerce. This would exclude some retail concerns and local jobbers and manufacturers not otherwise excluded from the operation of the act. Likewise banks and trust companies located in cities of less than 100,000 inhabitants might, if thought advisable, be excluded, for the present if their capital is less than $500,000, and their resources less than, say, $2,500,000. In larger cities even the smaller banking institutions should be subject to the law. Such exceptions should overcome any objection which might be raised that in some smaller cities, the prohibition of interlocking directorates would exclude from the bank directorates all the able business men of the community through fear of losing the opportunity of bank accommodations.

An exception should also be made, so as to permit interlocking directorates between a corporation and its proper subsidiaries. And the prohibition of transactions in which the management has a private interest should, of course, not apply to contracts, express or implied, for such services as are performed indiscriminately for the whole community by railroads and public service corporations, or for services, common to all customers, like the ordinary service of a bank for its depositors.

The Power of Congress

The question may be asked: Has Congress the power to impose these limitations upon the conduct of any business other than national banks? And if the power of Congress is so limited, will not the dominant financiers, upon the enactment of such a law, convert their national banks into state banks or trust companies, and thus escape from congressional control?

The answer to both questions is clear. Congress has ample power to impose such prohibitions upon practically all corporations, including state banks, trust companies, and life insurance companies; and evasion may be made impossible. While Congress has not been granted power to regulate *directly* state banks, and trust or life insurance companies, or railroad, public-service, and industrial corporations, except in respect to interstate commerce, it may do so *indirectly* by virtue either of its control of the mail privilege or through the taxing power.

Practically no business in the United States can be conducted without use of the mails; and Congress may in its reasonable discretion deny the use of the mail to any business which is conducted under conditions deemed by Congress to be injurious to the public welfare. Thus, Congress has no power directly to suppress lotteries; but it has indirectly suppressed them by denying, under heavy penalty, the use of the mail to lottery enterprises. Congress has no power to suppress directly business frauds; but it is constantly doing so indirectly by issuing fraud-orders denying the mail privilege. Congress has no direct power to require a newspaper to publish a list of its proprietors and the amount of its circulation, or to require it to mark paid-matter distinctly as advertising: But it has thus regulated the press, by denying the second-class mail privilege, to all publications which fail to comply with the requirements prescribed.

The taxing power has been resorted to by Congress for like purposes: Congress has no power to regulate the manufacture of matches, or the use of oleomargarine; but it has suppressed the manufacture of the "white phosphorous" match and has greatly lessened the use of oleomargarine by imposing heavy taxes upon them. Congress has no power to prohibit, or to regulate directly the issue of bank notes by state banks, but it indirectly prohibited their issue by imposing a tax of ten per cent. upon any bank note issued by a state bank.

The power of Congress over interstate commerce has been similarly utilized. Congress cannot ordinarily provide compensation for accidents to employees or undertake directly to suppress prostitution; but it has, as an incident of regulating interstate commerce, enacted the Railroad Employers' Liability law* and the White Slave Law; and it has full power over the instrumentalities of commerce, like the telegraph and the telephone.

As such exercise of congressional power has been common for, at least, half a century, Congress should not hesitate now to employ it where its exercise is urgently needed. For a comprehensive prohibition of interlocking directorates is an essential condition of our attaining the New Freedom. Such a law would involve a great change in the relation of the leading banks and bankers to other businesses. But it is the very purpose of Money Trust legislation to effect a great change; and unless it does so, the power of our financial oligarchy cannot be broken.

But though the enactment of such a law is essential to the emancipation of business, it will not *alone* restore industrial liberty. It must be supplemented by other remedial measures.

Chapter V

What Publicity Can Do

Publicity is justly commended as a remedy for social and industrial diseases. Sunlight is said to be the best of disinfectants; electric light the most efficient policeman. And publicity has already played an important part in the struggle against the Money Trust. The Pujo Committee has, in the disclosure of the facts concerning financial concentration, made a most important contribution toward attainment of the New Freedom. The battlefield has been surveyed and charted. The hostile forces have been located, counted, and appraised. That was a necessary first step—and a long one—towards relief. The provisions in the Committee's bill concerning the incorporation of stock exchanges and the statement to be made in connection with the listing of securities would doubtless have a beneficent effect. But there should be a further call upon publicity for service. That potent force must, in the impending struggle, be utilized in many ways as a continuous remedial measure.

*In the *Railroad Employers' Liability Act,* Congress had done away with a number of common law rules and redefined the liabilities railroads had when their workers were injured on the job; the Mann Act of 1910, or *White Slave Law,* had prohibited the transportation of women across state lines for immoral purposes and had been aimed at large-scale vice rings.

Wealth

Combination and control of other people's money and of other people's businesses. These are the main factors in the development of the Money Trust. But the wealth of the investment banker is also a factor. And with the extraordinary growth of his wealth in recent years, the relative importance of wealth as a factor in financial concentration has grown steadily. It was wealth which enabled Mr. Morgan, in 1910, to pay $3,000,000 for $51,000 par value of the stock of the Equitable Life Insurance Society. His direct income from this investment was limited by law to less than one-eighth of one per cent. a year; but it gave legal control of $504,000,000 of assets. It was wealth which enabled the Morgan associates to buy from the Equitable and the Mutual Life Insurance Company the stocks in the several banking institutions, which, merged in the Bankers' Trust Company and the Guaranty Trust Company, gave them control of $357,000,000 in deposits. It was wealth which enabled Mr. Morgan to acquire his shares in the First National and National City banks, worth $21,000,000, through which he cemented the triple alliance with those institutions.

Now, how has this great wealth been accumulated? Some of it was natural accretion. Some of it is due to special opportunities for investment wisely availed of. Some of it is due to the vast extent of the bankers' operations. Then power breeds wealth as wealth breeds power. But a main cause of these large fortunes is the huge tolls taken by those who control the avenues to capital and to investors. There has been exacted as toll literally "all that the traffic will bear."

Excessive Bankers' Commissions

The Pujo Committee was unfortunately prevented by lack of time from presenting to the country the evidence covering the amounts taken by the investment bankers as promoters' fees, underwriting commissions, and profits. Nothing could have demonstrated so clearly the power exercised by the bankers, as a schedule showing the aggregate of these taxes levied within recent years. It would be well worth while now to reopen the Money Trust investigation merely to collect these data. But earlier investigations have disclosed some illuminating, though sporadic facts.

The syndicate which promoted the Steel Trust, took, as compensation for a few weeks' work, securities yielding $62,500,000 in cash; and of this, J. P. Morgan & Co. received for their services, as Syndicate Managers, $12,500,000, besides their share, as syndicate subscribers, in the remaining $50,000,000. The Morgan syndicate took for promoting the Tube Trust $20,000,000 common stock out of a total issue of $80,000,000 stock (preferred and common). Nor were monster commissions limited to trust promotions. More recently, bankers' syndicates have, in many instances, received for floating preferred stocks of recapitalized industrial concerns, one-third of all common stock issued, besides a considerable sum in cash. And for the sale of preferred stock of well established manufacturing concerns, cash commissions (or profits) of from 7½ to 10 per cent. of the cash raised are often exacted. On bonds of high-class industrial concerns, bankers' commissions (or profits) of from 5 to 10 points have been common.

Nor have these heavy charges been confined to industrial concerns. Even railroad securities, supposedly of high grade, have been subjected to like burdens. At a time when the New Haven's credit was still unimpaired, J. P. Morgan & Co. took the New York, Westchester & Boston Railway first mortgage bonds, guaranteed by the New Haven at 92½; and they were marketed at 96¼. They took the Portland Terminal Company bonds, guaranteed by the Maine Central Railroad—a corporation of unquestionable credit—at about 88, and these were marketed at 92.

A large part of these underwriting commissions is taken by the great banking houses, not for their services in selling the bonds, nor in assuming risks, but for securing others to sell the bonds and incur risks. Thus when the Interboro Railway—a most prosperous corporation—financed its recent $170,000,000 bond issue, J. P. Morgan & Co. received a 3 per cent. commission, that is, $5,100,000, practically for arranging that others should underwrite and sell the bonds.

The aggregate commissions or profits so taken by leading banking houses can only be conjectured, as the full amount of their transactions has not been disclosed, and the rate of commission or profit varies very widely. But the Pujo Committee has supplied some interesting data bearing upon the subject: Counting the issues of securities of interstate corporations only, J. P. Morgan & Co. directly procured the public marketing alone or in conjunction with others during the years 1902–1912, of $1,950,000,000. What the average commission or profit taken by J. P. Morgan & Co. was we do not know; but we do know that every one per cent. on that sum yields $19,500,000. Yet even that huge aggregate of $1,950,000,000 includes only a part of the securities on which commissions or profits were paid. It does not include any issue of an intrastate corporation. It does not include any securities privately marketed. It does not include any government, state, or municipal bonds.

It is to exactions such as these that the wealth of the investment banker is in large part due. And since this wealth is an important factor in the creation of the power exercised by the Money Trust, we must endeavor to put an end to this improper wealth getting, as well as to improper combination. The Money Trust is so powerful and so firmly entrenched, that each of the sources of its undue power must be effectually stopped, if we would attain the New Freedom.

How Shall Excessive Charges Be Stopped?

The Pujo Committee recommends, as a remedy for such excessive charges, that interstate corporations be prohibited from entering into any agreements creating a sole fiscal agent to dispose of their security issues; that the issue of the securities of interstate railroads be placed under the supervision of the Interstate Commerce Commission; and that their securities should be disposed of only upon public or private competitive bids, or under regulations to be prescribed by the Commission with full powers of investigation that will discover and punish combinations which prevent competition in bidding. Some of the state public-service commissions now exercise such power; and it may possibly be wise to confer this power upon the interstate commission, although the recommendations of the Hadley Railroad Securities Commission are to the contrary. But the official regulation as proposed by the Pujo Committee would be confined to railroad corporations; and the new security issues of other corporations listed on the New York Stock Exchange have aggregated in the last five years $4,525,404,025, which is more than either the railroad or the municipal issues. Publicity offers, however, another and even more promising remedy: a method of regulating bankers' charges which would apply automatically to railroad, public-service, and industrial corporations alike.

The question may be asked: Why have these excessive charges been submitted to? Corporations, which in the first instance bear the charges for capital, have, doubtless, submitted because of banker-control; exercised directly through interlocking directorates, or kindred relations, and indirectly through combinations among bankers to suppress competition. But why have the investors submitted, since ultimately all these charges are borne by the investors, except so far as corporations succeed in shifting the burden upon the community? The large army of small investors, constituting a substantial majority of all security buyers, are entirely free from banker control. Their submission is undoubtedly due, in part, to the fact that the bankers control the avenues to recognized safe investments almost as fully as they do the avenues to capital. But the investor's servility is due partly, also, to his ignorance of the facts. Is it not probable that, if each investor knew the extent to which the security he buys from the banker is diluted by excessive underwritings, commissions, and profits, there would be a strike of capital against these unjust exactions?

The Strike of Capital

A recent British experience supports this view. In a brief period last spring nine different issues, aggregating $135,840,000, were offered by syndicates on the London market, and on the average only about 10 per cent. of these loans was taken by the public. Money was "tight," but the rates of interest offered were very liberal, and no one doubted that the investors were well supplied with funds. *The London Daily Mail* presented an explanation:

> The long series of rebuffs to new loans at the hands of investors reached a climax in the ill success of the great Rothschild issue. It will remain a topic of financial discussion for many days, and many in the city are expressing the opinion that it may have a revolutionary effect upon the present system of loan issuing and underwriting. The question being discussed is that the public have become loth to subscribe for stock which they believe the underwriters can afford, by reason of the commission they receive, to sell subsequently at a lower price than the issue price, and that the Stock Exchange has begun to realize the public's attitude. The public sees in the underwriter not so much one who insures that the loan shall be subscribed in return for its commission as a middleman, who, as it were, has an opportunity of obtaining stock at a lower price than the public in order that he may pass it off at a profit subsequently. They prefer not to subscribe, but to await an opportunity of dividing that profit. They feel that if, when these issues were made, the stock were offered them at a more attractive price, there would be less need to pay the underwriters so high commissions. It is another practical protest, if indirect, against the existence of the middleman, which protest is one of the features of present-day finance.

Publicity as a Remedy

Compel bankers when issuing securities to make public the commissions or profits they are receiving. Let every circular letter, prospectus or advertisement of a bond or stock show clearly what the banker received for his middleman-services, and what the bonds and stocks net the issuing corporation. That is knowledge to which both the existing security holder and the prospective purchaser are fairly entitled. If the bankers' compensation is reasonable, considering the skill and risk involved, there can be no objection to making it known. If it is not reasonable, the investor will "strike," as investors seem to have done recently in England.*

Such disclosures of bankers' commissions or profits is demanded also for another reason: It will aid the investor in judging of the safety of the investment. In the marketing of securities there are two classes of risks: One is the risk whether the banker (or the corporation) will find ready purchasers for the bonds or stock at the issue price; the other whether the investor will get a good article. The maker of the security and the banker are interested chiefly in getting it sold at the issue price. The investor is interested chiefly in buying a good article. The small investor relies almost exclusively upon the banker for his knowledge and judgment as to the quality of the security; and it is this which makes his relation to the banker one of confidence. But at present, the investment banker occupies a position inconsistent with that relation. The banker's compensation should, of course, vary according to the risk *he* assumes. Where there is a large risk that the bonds or stock will not be promptly sold at the issue price, the underwriting commission (that is the insurance premium) should be correspondingly large. But the banker ought not to be paid more for getting *investors* to assume a larger risk. In practice the banker gets the higher commission for underwriting the weaker security, on the ground that his own risk is greater. And the weaker the security, the greater is the banker's incentive to induce his customers to relieve him. Now the law should not undertake (except incidentally in connection with railroads and public-service corporations) to fix bankers' profits. And it should not seek to prevent investors from making bad bargains. But it is now recognized in the simplest merchandising, that there should be full disclosures. The archaic doctrine of *caveat emptor* is vanishing. The law has begun to require publicity in aid of fair dealing. The Federal Pure Food Law does not guarantee quality or prices; but it helps the buyer to judge of quality by requiring disclosure of ingredients. Among the most important facts to be learned for determining the real value of a security is the amount of water it contains. And any excessive amount paid to the banker for marketing a security is water. Require a full disclosure to the investor of the amount of commissions and profits paid; and not only will investors be put on their guard, but bankers' compensation will tend to adjust itself automatically to what is fair and reasonable. Excessive commissions—this form of unjustly acquired wealth—will in large part cease.

---

* Many of these measures were later enacted into law during the New Deal, and current securities regulations do in fact require the type of full disclosure Brandeis had called for in 1913.

Real Disclosure

But the disclosure must be real. And it must be a disclosure to the investor. It will not suffice to require merely the filing of a statement of facts with the Commissioner of Corporations or with a score of other officials, federal and state. That would be almost as ineffective as if the Pure Food Law required a manufacturer merely to deposit with the Department a statement of ingredients, instead of requiring the label to tell the story. Nor would the filing of a full statement with the Stock Exchange, if incorporated, as provided by the Pujo Committee bill, be adequate.

To be effective, knowledge of the facts must be actually brought home to the investor, and this can best be done by requiring the facts to be stated in good, large type in every notice, circular, letter, and advertisement inviting the investor to purchase. Compliance with this requirement should also be obligatory, and not something which the investor could waive. For the whole public is interested in putting an end to the bankers' exactions. England undertook, years ago, to protect its investors against the wiles of promoters, by requiring a somewhat similar disclosure; but the British act failed, in large measure of its purpose, partly because under it the statement of facts was filed only with a public official, and partly because the investor could waive the provision. And the British statute has now been changed in the latter respect.

Disclose Syndicate Particulars

The required publicity should also include a disclosure of all participants in an underwriting. It is a common incident of underwriting that no member of the syndicate shall sell at less than the syndicate price for a definite period, unless the syndicate is sooner dissolved. In other words, the bankers make, by agreement, an artificial price. Often the agreement is probably illegal under the Sherman Anti-Trust Law. This price maintenance is, however, not necessarily objectionable. It may be entirely consistent with the general welfare, if the facts are made known. But disclosure should include a list of those participating in the underwriting so that the public may not be misled. The investor should know whether his adviser is disinterested.

Not long ago a member of a leading banking house was undertaking to justify a commission taken by his firm for floating a now favorite preferred stock of a manufacturing concern. The bankers took for their services $250,000 in cash, besides one-third of the common stock, amounting to about $2,000,000. "Of course," he said, "that would have been too much if we could have kept it all for ourselves; but we couldn't. We had to divide up a large part. There were fifty-seven participants. Why, we had even to give $10,000 of stock to —— (naming the president of a leading bank in the city where the business was located). He might some day have been asked what he thought of the stock. If he had shrugged his shoulders and said he didn't know, we might have lost many a customer for the stock. We had to give him $10,000 of the stock to teach him not to shrug his shoulders."

Think of the effectiveness with practical Americans of a statement like this:

A. B. & CO.

INVESTMENT BANKERS

We have today secured substantial control of the successful machinery business heretofore conducted by —— at ——, Illinois, which has been incorporated under the name of the Excelsior Manufacturing Company with a capital of $10,000,000, of which $5,000,000 is Preferred and $5,000,000 Common.

As we have a large clientele of confiding customers, we were able to secure from the owners an agreement for marketing the Preferred stock — we to fix a price which shall net the owners in cash $95 a share.

We offer this excellent stock to you at $100.75 per share. Our own commission or profit will be only a little over $5.00 per share, or say, $250,000 cash, besides $1,500,000 of the Common stock, which we received as a bonus. This cash and stock commission we are to divide in various proportions with the following participants in the underwriting syndicate:

C. D. & Co., New York
E. F. & Co., Boston
L. M. & Co., Philadelphia
I. K. & Co., New York
O. P. & Co., Chicago

Were such notices common, the investment bankers would "be worthy of their hire," for only reasonable compensation would ordinarily be taken.

For marketing the preferred stock, as in the case of Excelsior Manufacturing Co. referred to above, investment bankers were doubtless essential, and as middlemen they performed a useful service. But they used their strong position to make an excessive charge. There are, however, many cases where the banker's services can be altogether dispensed with; and where that is possible he should be eliminated, not only for economy's sake, but to break up financial concentration.

Chapter VI

Where the Banker Is Superfluous

The abolition of interlocking directorates will greatly curtail the bankers' power by putting an end to many improper combinations. Publicity concerning bankers' commissions, profits, and associates, will lend effective aid, particularly by curbing undue exactions. Many of the specific measures recommended by the Pujo Committee (some of them dealing with technical details) will go far toward correcting corporate and banking abuses; and thus tend to arrest financial concentration. But the investment banker has, within his legitimate province, acquired control so extensive as to menace the public welfare, even where his business is properly conducted. If the New Freedom is to be attained, every proper means of lessening that power must be availed of. A simple and effective remedy, which can be widely applied, even without new legislation, lies near at hand: — Eliminate the banker-middleman where he is superfluous.

Today practically all governments, states, and municipalities pay toll to the banker on all bonds sold. Why should they? It is not because the banker is always needed. It is because the banker controls the only avenue through which the investor in bonds and stocks can ordinarily be reached. The banker has become the universal tax gatherer. True, the *pro rata* of taxes levied by him upon our state and city governments is less than that levied by him upon the corporations. But few states or cities escape payment of some such tax to the banker on every loan it makes. Even where the new issues of bonds are sold at public auction, or to the highest bidder on sealed proposals, the bankers' syndicates usually secure large blocks of the bonds which are sold to the people at a considerable profit. The middleman, even though unnecessary, collects his tribute.

There is a legitimate field for dealers in state and municipal bonds, as for other merchants. Investors already owning such bonds must have a medium through which they can sell their holdings. And those states or municipalities which lack an established reputation among investors, or which must seek more distant markets, need the banker to distribute new issues. But there are many states and cities which have an established reputation and have a home market at hand. These should sell their bonds direct to investors without the intervention of a middleman. And as like conditions prevail with some corporations, their bonds and stocks should also be sold direct to the investor. Both financial efficiency and industrial liberty demand that the bankers' toll be abolished, where that is possible.

Banker and Broker

The business of the investment banker must not be confused with that of the bond and stock broker. The two are often combined; but the functions are essentially different. The broker performs a very limited service. He has properly nothing to do with the original issue of securities, nor with their introduction into the market. He merely negotiates a purchase or sale as agent for another under specific orders. He exercises no discretion, except in the method of bringing buyer and seller together, or of executing orders. For his humble service he receives a moderate compensation, a commission, usually one-eighth of one per cent. (12½ cents for each $100) on the par value of the security sold. The investment banker also is a mere middleman. But he is a principal, not an agent. He is also a merchant in bonds and stocks. The compensation received for his part in the transaction is in many cases more accurately described as profit than as commission. So far as concerns new issues of government, state, and municipal bonds, especially, he acts as merchant, buying and selling securities on his own behalf; buying commonly at wholesale from the maker and selling at retail to the investors; taking the merchant's risk and the merchant's profits. On purchases of corporate securities the profits are often very large; but even a large profit may be entirely proper; for when the banker's services are needed and are properly performed, they are of great value. On purchases of government, state, and municipal securities the profit is usually smaller; but even a very small profit cannot be justified, if unnecessary.

How the Banker Can Serve

The banker's services include three distinct functions, and only three:

First: Specifically as expert. The investment banker has the responsibility of the ordinary retailer to sell only that merchandise which is good of its kind. But his responsibility in this respect is unusually heavy, because he deals in an article on which a great majority of his customers are unable, themselves, to pass intelligent judgment without aid. The purchase by the investor of most corporate securities is little better than a gamble, where he fails to get the advice of some one who has investigated the security thoroughly as the banker should. For few investors have the time, the facilities, or the ability to investigate properly the value of corporate securities.

Second: Specifically as distributor. The banker performs an all-important service in providing an outlet for securities. His connections enable him to reach possible buyers quickly. And good-will—that is, possession of the confidence of regular customers—enables him to effect sales where the maker of the security might utterly fail to find a market. *Third:* Specifically as jobber or retailer. The investment banker, like other merchants, carries his stock in trade until it can be marketed. In this he performs a service which is often of great value to the maker. Needed cash is obtained immediately, because the whole issue of securities can thus be disposed of by a single transaction. And even where there is not immediate payment, the knowledge that the money will be provided when needed is often of paramount importance. By carrying securities in stock, the banker performs a service also to investors, who are thereby enabled to buy securities at such times as they desire.

Whenever makers of securities or investors require all or any of these three services, the investment banker is needed, and payment of compensation to him is proper. Where there is no such need, the banker is clearly superfluous. And in respect to the original issue of many of our state and municipal bonds, and of some corporate securities, no such need exists.

Where the Banker Serves Not

It needs no banker experts in value to tell us that bonds of Massachusetts or New York, of Boston, Philadelphia, or Baltimore, and of scores of lesser American cities, are safe investments. The basic financial facts in regard to such bonds are a part of the common knowledge of many American investors; and, certainly, of most possible investors who reside in the particular state or city whose bonds are in question. Where the financial facts are not generally known, they are so simple, that they can be easily summarized and understood by any prospective investor without interpretation by an expert. Bankers often employ, before purchasing securities, their own accountants to verify the statements supplied by the makers of the security, and use these accountants' certificates as an aid in selling. States and municipalities, the makers of the securities, might for the same purpose employ independent public accountants of high reputation, who would give their certificates for use in marketing the securities. Investors could also be assured without banker-aid that the basic legal conditions are sound. Bankers, before purchasing an issue of securities, customarily obtain from their own counsel an opinion as to its legality, which investors are invited to examine. It would answer the same purpose, if states and municipalities should supplement the opinion of their legal representatives by that of independent counsel of recognized professional standing, who would certify to the legality of the issue.

Neither should an investment banker be needed to find investors willing to take up, in small lots, a new issue of bonds of New York or Massachusetts, of Boston, Philadelphia or Baltimore, or a hundred other American cities. A state or municipality seeking to market direct to the investor its own bonds would naturally experience, at the outset, some difficulty in marketing a large issue. And in a newer community, where there is little accumulation of unemployed capital, it might be impossible to find buyers for any large issue. Investors are apt to be conservative; and they have been trained to regard the intervention of the banker as necessary. The bankers would naturally discourage any attempt of states and cities to dispense with their services. Entrance upon a market, hitherto monopolized by them, would usually have to be struggled for. But banker-fed investors, as well as others could, in time, be brought to realize the advantage of avoiding the middleman and dealing directly with responsible borrowers. Governments, like private concerns, would have to do educational work; but this publicity would be much less expensive and much more productive than that undertaken by the bankers. Many investors are already impatient of banker exactions; and eager to deal directly with governmental agencies in whom they have more confidence. And a great demand could, at once, be developed among smaller investors whom the bankers have been unable to interest, and who now never buy state or municipal bonds. The opening of this new field would furnish a market, in some respects more desirable and certainly wider than that now reached by the bankers.

Neither do states or cities ordinarily need the services of the investment banker to carry their bonds pending distribution to the investor. Where there is immediate need for large funds, states and cities—at least the older communities—should be able to raise the money temporarily, quite as well as the bankers do now, while awaiting distribution of their bonds to the investor. Bankers carry the bonds with other people's money, not their own. Why should not cities get the temporary use of other people's money as well? Bankers have the preferential use of the deposits in the banks, often because they control the banks. Free these institutions from banker-control, and no applicant to borrow the people's money will be received with greater favor than our large cities. Boston, with its $1,500,000,000 of assessed valuation and $78,033,128 net debt, is certainly as good a risk as even Lee, Higginson & Co. or Kidder, Peabody & Co.

But ordinarily cities do not, or should not, require large sums of money at any one time. Such need of large sums does not arise except from time to time where maturing loans are to be met, or when some existing public utility plant is to be taken over from private owners. Large issues of bonds for any other purpose are usually made in anticipation of future needs, rather than to meet present necessities. Modern efficient public financiering, through substituting serial bonds for the long term issues (which in Massachusetts has been made obligatory) will, in time, remove the need of large sums at one time for paying maturing debts, since each year's maturities will be paid from the year's taxes. Purchases of existing public utility plants are of rare occurrence, and are apt to be preceded by long periods of negotiation. When they occur they can, if foresight be exercised, usually be financed without full cash payment at one time.

Today, when a large issue of bonds is made, the banker, while ostensibly paying his own money to the city, actually pays to the city other people's money which he has borrowed from the banks. Then the banks get back, through the city's deposits, a large part of the money so received. And when the money is returned to the bank, the banker has the opportunity of borrowing it again for other operations. The process results in double loss to the city. The city loses by not getting from the banks as much for its bonds as investors would pay. And then it loses interest on the money raised before it is needed. For the bankers receive from the city bonds bearing rarely less than 4 per cent. interest; while the proceeds are deposited in the banks which rarely allow more than 2 per cent. interest on the daily balances.

Cities That Helped Themselves

In the present year some cities have been led by necessity to help themselves. The bond market was poor. Business was uncertain, money tight, and the ordinary investor reluctant. Bankers were loth to take new bond issues. Municipalities were unwilling to pay the high rates demanded of them. And many cities were prohibited by law or ordinance from paying more than 4 per cent. interest; while good municipal bonds were then selling on a 4½ to 5 per cent. basis. But money had to be raised, and the attempt was made to borrow it direct from the lenders instead of from the banker-middleman. Among the cities which raised money in this way were Philadelphia, Baltimore, St. Paul, and Utica, New York.

Philadelphia, under Mayor Blankenburg's inspiration, sold nearly $4,175,000 in about two days on a 4 per cent. basis and another "over-the-counter" sale has been made since. In Baltimore, with the assistance of the *Sun*, $4,766,000 were sold "over the counter" on a 4½ per cent.

basis. Utica's two "popular sales" of 4½ per cent. bonds were largely "over-subscribed." And since then other cities large and small have had their "over-the-counter" bond sales. The experience of Utica, as stated by its Controller, Fred G. Reusswig, must prove of general interest:

In June of the present year I advertised for sale two issues, one of $100,000, and the other of $19,000, bearing interest at 4½ per cent. The latter issue was purchased at par by a local bidder and of the former we purchased $10,000 for our sinking funds. That left $90,000 unsold, for which there were no bidders, which was the first time that I had been unable to sell our bonds. About this time the "popular sales" of Baltimore and Philadelphia attracted my attention. The laws in effect in those cities did not restrict the officials as does our law and I could not copy their methods. I realized that there was plenty of money in this immediate vicinity and if I could devise a plan conforming with our laws under which I could make the sale attractive to small investors it would undoubtedly prove successful. I had found, in previous efforts to interest people of small means, that they did not understand the meaning of premium and would rather not buy than bid above par. They also objected to making a deposit with their bids. In arranging for the "popular sales" I announced in the papers that, while I must award to the highest bidder, it was my opinion that a par bid would be *the highest bid*. I also announced that we would issue bonds in denominations as low as $100 and that we would not require a deposit except where the bid was $5,000 or over. Then I succeeded in getting the local papers to print editorials and local notices upon the subject of municipal bonds, with particular reference to those of Utica and the forthcoming sale. All the prospective purchaser had to do was to fill in the amount desired, sign his name, seal the bid, and await the day for the award. I did not have many bidders for very small amounts. There was only one for $100 at the first sale and one for $100 at the second sale and not more than ten who wanted less than $500. Most of the bidders were looking for from $1,000 to $5,000, but nearly all were people of comparatively small means, and with some the investment represented all their savings. In awarding the bonds I gave preference to residents of Utica and I had no difficulty in apportioning the various maturities in a satisfactory way.

I believe that there are a large number of persons in every city who would buy their own bonds if the way were made easier by law. Syracuse and the neighboring village of Ilion, both of which had been unable to sell in the usual way, came to me for a program of procedure and both have since had successful sales along similar lines. We have been able by this means to keep the interest rate on our bonds at 4½ per cent., while cities which have followed the old plan of relying upon bond houses have had to increase the rate to 5 per cent. I am in favor of amending the law in such a manner that the Common Council, approved by the Board of Estimate and Apportionment, may fix the prices at which bonds shall be sold, instead of calling for competitive bids. Then place the bonds on sale at the Controller's office to any one who will pay the price. The prices upon each issue should be graded according to the different values of different maturities. Under the present law, as we have it, conditions are too complicated to make a sale practicable except upon a basis of par bids.

The St. Paul Experiment

St. Paul wisely introduced into its experiment a more democratic feature, which Tom L. Johnson, Cleveland's mayor, thought out (but did not utilize), and which his friend W. B. Colver, now Editor-in-Chief of the *Daily News,* brought to the attention of the St. Paul officials. Mayor Johnson had recognized the importance of reaching the small savings of the people; and concluded that it was necessary not only to issue the bonds in very small denominations, but also to make them redeemable at par. He sought to combine practically, bond investment with the savings bank privilege. The fact that municipal bonds are issuable ordinarily only in large denominations, say, $1,000, presented an obstacle to be overcome. Mayor Johnson's plan was to have the sinking fund commissioners take large blocks of the bonds, issue against them certificates in denominations of $10, and have the commissioners agree (under their power to purchase securities) to buy the certificates back at par and interest. Savings bank experience, he insisted, showed that the redemption feature would not prove an embarrassment; as the percentage of those wishing to withdraw their money is small; and deposits are nearly always far in excess of withdrawals.

The St. Paul sinking fund commissioners and City Attorney O'Neill approved the Johnson plan; and in the face of high money rates, sold on a 4 per cent. basis, during July, certificates to the net amount of $502,300; during August, $147,000; and during September, over $150,000, the average net sales being about $5,700 a day. Mr. Colver, reporting on the St. Paul experience, said:

> There have been about 2,000 individual purchasers making the average deposit about $350 or $360. There have been no certificates sold to banks. During the first month the deposits averaged considerably higher and for this reason: in very many cases people who had savings which represented the accumulation of considerable time, withdrew their money from the postal savings banks, from the regular banks, from

various hiding places and deposited them with the city. Now these same people are coming once or twice a month and making deposits of ten or twenty dollars, so that the average of the individual deposit has fallen very rapidly during September and every indication is that the number of small deposits will continue to increase and the relatively large deposits become less frequent as time goes on.

As a matter of fact, these certificate deposits are stable, far more than the deposits and investments of richer people who watch for advantageous reinvestments and who shift their money about rather freely. The man with three or four hundred dollars savings will suffer almost anything before he will disturb that fund. We believe that the deposits every day here, day in and day out, will continue to take care of all the withdrawals and still leave a net gain for the day, that net figure at present being about $5,700 a day.

Many cities are now prevented from selling bonds direct to the small investors, through laws which compel bonds to be issued in large denominations or which require the issue to be offered to the highest bidder. These legislative limitations should be promptly removed.

Salesmanship and Education

Such success as has already been attained is largely due to the unpaid educational work of leading progressive newspapers. But the educational work to be done must not be confined to teaching "the people" — the buyers of the bonds. Municipal officials and legislators have quite as much to learn. They must, first of all, study salesmanship. Selling bonds to the people is a new art, still undeveloped. The general problems have not yet been worked out. And besides these problems common to all states and cities, there will be, in nearly every community, local problems which must be solved, and local difficulties which must be overcome. The proper solution even of the general problems must take considerable time. There will have to be many experiments made; and doubtless there will be many failures. Every great distributor of merchandise knows the obstacles which he had to overcome before success was attained; and the large sums that had to be invested in opening and preparing a market. Individual concerns have spent millions in wise publicity; and have ultimately reaped immense profits when the market was won. Cities must take their lessons from these great distributors. Cities must be ready to study the problems and to spend prudently for proper publicity work. It might, in the end, prove an economy, even to allow, on particular issues, where necessary, a somewhat higher interest rate than bankers would exact, if thereby a direct market for bonds could be secured. Future operations would yield large economies. And the obtaining of a direct market for city bonds is growing ever more important, because of the huge increase in loans which must attend the constant expansion of municipal functions. In 1898 the new municipal issues aggregated $103,084,793; in 1912, $380,810,287.

Savings Banks as Customers

In New York, Massachusetts, and the other sixteen states where a system of purely mutual savings banks is general, it is possible, with a little organization, to develop an important market for the direct purchaser of bonds. The bonds issued by Massachusetts cities and towns have averaged recently about $15,000,000 a year, and those of the state about $3,000,000. The 194 Massachusetts savings banks, with aggregate assets of $902,105,755.94, held on October 31, 1912, $90,536,581.32 in bonds and notes of states and municipalities. Of this sum about $60,000,000 are invested in bonds and notes of Massachusetts cities and towns, and about $8,000,000 in state issues. The deposits in the savings banks are increasing at the rate of over $30,000,000 a year. Massachusetts state and municipal bonds have, within a few years, come to be issued tax exempt in the hands of the holder, whereas other classes of bonds usually held by savings banks are subject to a tax of one-half of one per cent. of the market value. Massachusetts savings banks, therefore, will to an increasing extent, select Massachusetts municipal issues for high-grade bond investments. Certainly Massachusetts cities and towns might, with the cooperation of the Commonwealth, easily develop a "home market" for "over-the-counter" bond business with the savings banks. And the savings banks of other states offer similar opportunities to their municipalities.

Cooperation

Bankers obtained their power through combination. Why should not cities and states by means of cooperation free themselves from the bankers? For by cooperation between the cities and the state, the direct marketing of municipal bonds could be greatly facilitated.

Massachusetts has 33 cities, each with a population of over 12,000 persons; 71 towns each with a population of over 5,000; and 250 towns each with a population of less than 5,000. Three hundred and eight of these municipalities now have funded indebtedness outstanding. The aggregate net indebtedness is about $180,000,000. Every year about $15,000,000 of bonds and notes are issued by the Massachusetts cities and towns for the purpose of meeting new requirements and refunding old indebtedness. If these municipalities would cooperate in marketing securities, the market for the bonds of each municipality would be widened; and there would exist also a common market for Massachusetts municipal securities which would be usually well supplied, would receive proper publicity, and would attract investors. Successful merchandising obviously involves carrying an adequate, well-assorted stock. If every city acts alone, in endeavoring to market its bonds direct, the city's bond-selling activity will necessarily be sporadic. Its ability to supply the investor will be limited by its own necessities for money. The market will also be limited to the bonds of the particular municipality. But if a state and its cities should cooperate, there could be developed a continuous and broad market for the sale of bonds "over-the-counter." The joint selling agency of over three hundred municipalities—as in Massachusetts—would naturally have a constant supply of assorted bonds and notes which could be had in as small amounts as the investor might want to buy them. It would be a simple matter to establish such a joint selling agency by which municipalities, under proper regulation of, and aid from the state, would cooperate.

And cooperation among the cities and with the state might serve in another important respect. These 354 Massachusetts municipalities carry in the aggregate large bank balances. Sometimes the balance carried by a city represents unexpended revenues; sometimes unexpended proceeds of loans. On these balances they usually receive from the banks 2 per cent. interest. The balances of municipalities vary like those of other depositors; one having idle funds, when another is in need. Why should not all of these cities and towns cooperate, making, say, the State their common banker, and supply each other with funds as farmers and laborers cooperate through credit unions?* Then cities would get, instead of 2 per cent. on their balances, all their money was worth.

The Commonwealth of Massachusetts holds now in its sinking and other funds nearly $30,000,000 of Massachusetts municipal securities, constituting nearly three-fourths of all securities held in these funds. Its annual purchases aggregate nearly $4,000,000. Its purchases direct from cities and towns have already exceeded $1,000,000 this year. It would be but a simple extension of the state's function to cooperate, as indicated, in a joint, Municipal Bond Selling Agency and Credit Union. It would be a distinct advance in the efficiency of state and municipal financing; and what is even more important, a long step toward the emancipation of the people from banker-control.

Credit unions are cooperative savings and loan associations that make loans to their members at low interest rates.

Corporate Self-help

Strong corporations with established reputations, locally or nationally, could emancipate themselves from the banker in a similar manner. Public-service corporations in some of our leading cities could easily establish "over-the-counter" home markets for their bonds; and would be greatly aided in this by the supervision now being exercised by some state commissions over the issue of securities by such corporations. Such corporations would gain thereby not only in freedom from banker-control and exactions, but in the winning of valuable local support. The investor's money would be followed by his sympathy. In things economic, as well as in things political, wisdom and safety lie in direct appeals to the people.

The Pennsylvania Railroad now relies largely upon its stockholders for new capital. But a corporation with its long-continued success and reputation for stability should have much wider financial support and should eliminate the banker altogether. With the 2,700 stations on its system, the Pennsylvania could, with a slight expense, create nearly as many avenues through which money would be obtainable to meet its growing needs.

Banker Protectors

It may be urged that reputations often outlive the conditions which justify them, that outlived reputations are pitfalls to the investors; and that the investment banker is needed to guard him from such dangers. True; but when have the big bankers or their little satellites protected the people from such pitfalls?

Was there ever a more be-bankered railroad than the New Haven?* Was there ever a more banker-led community of investors than New England? Six years before the fall of that great system, the hidden dangers were pointed out to these banker-experts. Proof was furnished of the rotting timbers. The disaster-breeding policies were laid bare. The bankers took no action. Repeatedly, thereafter, the bankers' attention was called to the steady deterioration of the structure. The New Haven books disclose 11,481 stockholders who are residents of Massachusetts; 5,682 stockholders in Connecticut; 735 in Rhode Island; and 3,510 in New York. Of the New Haven stockholders 10,474 were women. Of the New Haven stockholders 10,222 were of such modest means that their holdings were

---

* The *fall of the New Haven system* had occurred on grounds that Brandeis had predicted in his fight against the merger of the New Haven and Boston & Maine lines. He argued that the new line would be terribly overextended and would not be able to earn enough to pay the large debt incurred in the Morgan-sponsored merger.

from one to ten shares only. The investors were sorely in need of protection. The city directories disclose 146 banking houses in Boston, 26 in Providence, 33 in New Haven and Hartford, and 357 in New York City. But who, connected with those New England and New York banking houses, during the long years which preceded the recent investigation of the Interstate Commerce Commission, raised either voice or pen in protest against the continuous mismanagement of that great trust property or warned the public of the impending disaster? Some of the bankers sold their own stock holdings. Some bankers whispered to a few favored customers advice to dispose of New Haven stock. But not one banker joined those who sought to open the eyes of New England to the impending disaster and to avert it by timely measures. New England's leading banking houses were ready to "cooperate" with the New Haven management in taking generous commissions for marketing the endless supply of new securities; but they did nothing to protect the investors. Were these bankers blind? Or were they afraid to oppose the will of J. P. Morgan & Co.?

Perhaps it is the banker who, most of all, needs the New Freedom.

Chapter VII

Big Men and Little Business

J. P. Morgan & Co. declare, in their letter to the Pujo Committee, that "practically all the railroad and industrial development of this country has taken place initially through the medium of the great banking houses." That statement is entirely unfounded in fact. On the contrary nearly every such contribution to our comfort and prosperity was "initiated" *without* their aid. The "great banking houses" came into relation with these enterprises, either after success had been attained, or upon "reorganization" after the possibility of success had been demonstrated, but the funds of the hardy pioneers, who had risked their all, were exhausted.

This is true of our early railroads, of our early street railways, and of the automobile; of the telegraph, the telephone, and the wireless; of gas and oil; of harvesting machinery, and of our steel industry; of the textile, paper, and shoe industries; and of nearly every other important branch of manufacture. The *initiation* of each of these enterprises may properly be characterized as "great transactions"; and the men who contributed the financial aid and business management necessary for their introduction are entitled to share, equally with inventors, in our gratitude for what has been accomplished. But the instances are extremely rare where the original financing of such enterprises was undertaken by investment bankers, great or small. It was usually done by some common business man, accustomed to taking risks; or by some well-to-do friend of the inventor or pioneer, who was influenced largely by considerations other than money-getting. Here and there you will find that banker-aid was given; but usually in those cases it was a small local banking concern, not a "great banking house" which helped to "initiate" the undertaking.

Railroads

We have come to associate the great bankers with railroads. But their part was not conspicuous in the early history of the Eastern railroads; and in the Middle West the experience was, to some extent, similar. The Boston & Maine Railroad owns and leases 2,215 miles of line; but it is a composite of about 166 separate railroad companies. The New Haven Railroad owns and leases 1,996 miles of line; but it is a composite of 112 separate railroad companies. The necessary capital to build these little roads was gathered together, partly through state, county, or municipal aid; partly from business men or landholders who sought to advance their special interests; partly from investors; and partly from well-to-do public-spirited men, who wished to promote the welfare of their particular communities. About seventy-five years after the first of these railroads was built, J. P. Morgan & Co. became fiscal agent for all of them by creating the New Haven–Boston & Maine monopoly.

Steamships

The history of our steamship lines is similar. In 1807, Robert Fulton, with the financial aid of Robert R. Livingston, a judge and statesman—not a banker—demonstrated with the *Claremont,* that it was practicable to propel boats by steam. In 1833 the three Cunard brothers of Halifax and 232 other persons—stockholders of the Quebec and Halifax Steam Navigation Company—joined in supplying about $80,000 to build the *Royal William*—the first steamer to cross the Atlantic. In 1902, many years after individual enterprises had developed practically all the great ocean lines, J. P. Morgan & Co. floated the International Mercantile Marine with its $52,744,000 of 4½ bonds, now selling at about 60, and $100,000,000 of stock (preferred and common) on which no dividend has ever been paid. It was just sixty-two years after the first regular line of transatlantic steamers—The Cunard—was founded that Mr. Morgan organized the Shipping Trust.

Telegraph

The story of the telegraph is similar. The money for developing Morse's* invention was supplied by his partner and co-worker, Alfred Vail. The initial line (from Washington to Baltimore) was built with an appropriation of $30,000 made by Congress in 1843. Sixty-six years later J. P. Morgan & Co. became bankers for the Western Union through financing its purchase by the American Telephone & Telegraph Company.

Harvesting Machinery

Next to railroads and steamships, harvesting machinery has probably been the most potent factor in the development of America; and most important of the harvesting machines was Cyrus H. McCormick's reaper. That made it possible to increase the grain harvest twenty- or thirty-fold. No investment banker had any part in introducing this great business man's invention.

McCormick was without means; but William Butler Ogden, a railroad builder, ex-Mayor and leading citizen of Chicago, supplied $25,000 with which the first factory was built there in 1847. Fifty-five years later, J. P. Morgan & Co. performed the service of combining the five great harvester companies, and received a commission of $3,000,000. The concerns then consolidated as the International Harvester Company, with a capital stock of $120,000,000, had, despite their huge assets and earning power, been previously capitalized, in the aggregate, at only $10,500,000—strong evidence that in all the preceding years no investment banker had financed them. Indeed, McCormick was as able in business as in mechanical invention. Two years after Ogden paid him $25,000 for a half interest in the business, McCormick bought it back for $50,000; and thereafter, until his death in 1884, no one but members of the McCormick family had any interest in the business.

The Banker Era

It may be urged that railroads and steamships, the telegraph, and harvesting machinery were introduced before the accumulation of investment capital had developed the investment banker, and before America's "great

---

Samuel F. B. Morse invented the telegraph in the 1840s.

banking houses" had been established; and that, consequently, it would be fairer to inquire what services bankers had rendered in connection with later industrial development. The firm of J. P. Morgan & Co. is fifty-five years old; Kuhn, Loeb & Co. fifty-six years old; Lee, Higginson & Co. over fifty years; and Kidder, Peabody & Co. forty-eight years; and yet the investment banker seems to have had almost as little part in "initiating" the great improvements of the last half century, as did bankers in the earlier period.

Steel

The modern steel industry of America is forty-five years old. The "great bankers" had no part in initiating it. Andrew Carnegie, then already a man of large means, introduced the Bessemer process* in 1868. In the next thirty years our steel and iron industry increased greatly. By 1898 we had far outstripped all competitors. America's production about equaled the aggregate of England and Germany. We had also reduced costs so much that Europe talked of the "American Peril."** It was 1898, when J. P. Morgan & Co. took their first step in forming the Steel Trust, by organizing the Federal Steel Company. Then followed the combination of the tube mills into an $80,000,000 corporation, J. P. Morgan & Co. taking for their syndicate services $20,000,000 of common stock. About the same time the consolidation of the bridge and structural works, the tin plate, the sheet steel, the hoop, and other mills followed; and finally, in 1901, the Steel Trust was formed, with a capitalization of $1,402,000,000. These combinations came thirty years after the steel industry had been "initiated."

The Telephone

The telephone industry is less than forty years old. It is probably America's greatest contribution to industrial development. The bankers had no part in "initiating" it. The glory belongs to a simple, enthusiastic, warmhearted business man of Haverhill, Massachusetts, who was willing to risk *his own* money. H. N. Casson tells of this, most interestingly, in his "History of the Telephone":

---

*The *Bessemer process* was developed by an Englishman, Sir Henry Bessemer, in the 1870s and employed a process to transform molten iron into steel. Prior to Bessemer, steel was expensive to make, and his process revolutionized the industry.

** By *"the American Peril"* European manufacturers meant they feared that inexpensive American-made goods might drive their products from the world markets.

The only man who had money and dared to stake it on the future of the telephone was Thomas Sanders, and he did this not mainly for business reasons. Both he and Hubbard were attached to Bell* primarily by sentiment, as Bell had removed the blight of dumbness from Sanders' little son, and was soon to marry Hubbard's daughter. Also, Sanders had no expectation, at first, that so much money would be needed. He was not rich. His entire business, which was that of cutting out soles for shoe manufacturers, was not at any time worth more than thirty-five thousand dollars. Yet, from 1874 to 1878, he had advanced nine-tenths of the money that was spent on the telephone. The first five thousand telephones, and more, were made with his money. And so many long, expensive months dragged by before any relief came to Sanders, that he was compelled, much against his will and his business judgment, to stretch his credit within an inch of the breaking-point to help Bell and the telephone. Desperately he signed note after note until he faced a total of one hundred and ten thousand dollars. If the new "scientific toy" succeeded, which he often doubted, he would be the richest citizen in Haverhill; and if it failed, which he sorely feared, he would be a bankrupt. Sanders and Hubbard were leasing telephones two by two, to business men who previously had been using the private lines of the Western Union Telegraph Company. This great corporation was at this time their natural and inevitable enemy. It had swallowed most of its competitors, and was reaching out to monopolize all methods of communication by wire. The rosiest hope that shone in front of Sanders and Hubbard was that the Western Union might conclude to buy the Bell patents, just as it had already bought many others. In one moment of discouragement they had offered the telephone to President Orton, of the Western Union, for $100,000; and Orton had refused it. "What use," he asked pleasantly, "could this company make of an electrical toy?"

But besides the operation of its own wires, the Western Union was supplying customers with various kinds of printing-telegraphs and dial-telegraphs, some of which could transmit sixty words a minute. These accurate instruments, it believed, could never be displaced by such a scientific oddity as the telephone, and it continued to believe this until one of its subsidiary companies—the Gold and Stock—reported that several of its machines had been superseded by telephones.

At once the Western Union awoke from its indifference. Even this tiny nibbling at its business must be stopped. It took action quickly, and organized the "American Speaking-Telephone Company," and with $300,000 capital, and with three electrical inventors, Edison, Gray, and Dolbear, on its staff. With all the bulk of its great wealth and prestige, it swept down upon Bell and his little body-guard. It trampled upon Bell's patent with as little concern as an elephant can have when he tramples

---

Alexander Graham Bell was the inventor of the telephone.

upon an ant's nest. To the complete bewilderment of Bell, it coolly announced that it had the only original telephone, and that it was ready to supply superior telephones with all the latest improvements made by the original inventors—Dolbear, Gray, and Edison.*

The result was strange and unexpected. The Bell group, instead of being driven from the field, were at once lifted to a higher level in the business world. And the Western Union, in the endeavor to protect its private lines, became involuntarily a "bell-wether" to lead capitalists in the direction of the telephone.

Even then, when financial aid came to the Bell enterprise, it was from capitalists, not from bankers, and among these capitalists was William H. Forbes (son of the builder of the Burlington) who became the first President of the Bell Telephone Company. That was in 1878. More than twenty years later, after the telephone had spread over the world, the great house of Morgan came into financial control of the property. The American Telephone & Telegraph Company was formed. The process of combination became active. Since January, 1900, its stock has increased from $25,886,300 to $344,606,400. In six years (1906 to 1912), the Morgan associates marketed about $300,000,000 bonds of that company or its subsidiaries. In that period the volume of business done by the telephone companies had, of course, grown greatly, and the plant had to be constantly increased; but the proceeds of these huge security issues were used, to a large extent, in effecting combinations; that is, in buying out telephone competitors; in buying control of the Western Union Telegraph Company; and in buying up outstanding stock interests in semi-independent Bell companies. It is these combinations which have led to the investigation of the Telephone Company by the Department of Justice; and they are, in large part, responsible for the movement to have the government take over the telephone business.

Electrical Machinery

The business of manufacturing electrical machinery and apparatus is only a little over thirty years old. J. P. Morgan & Co. became interested early in one branch of it; but their dominance of the business today is due, not to their "initiating" it, but to their effecting a combination, and organizing the General Electric Company in 1892. There were then three large electrical

---

* *Thomas Edison,* of course, was the great inventor whose work was at the heart of much modern electrical technology; *Elisha Gray* was an inventor and the head of Western Electric; *Amos Emerson Dolbear,* a professor of physics at Tufts, was also an inventor and held a number of patents in telephony and telegraphy.

companies, the Thomson-Houston, the Edison, and the Westinghouse, besides some small ones. The Thomson-Houston of Lynn, Massachusetts, was in many respects the leader, having been formed to introduce, among other things, important inventions of Prof. Elihu Thomson and Prof. Houston. Lynn is one of the principal shoe-manufacturing centers of America. It is within ten miles of State Street, Boston; but Thomson's early financial support came not from Boston bankers, but mainly from Lynn business men and investors; men active, energetic, and used to taking risks with *their own* money. Prominent among them was Charles A. Coffin, a shoe manufacturer, who became connected with the Thomson-Houston Company upon its organization and president of the General Electric when Mr. Morgan formed that company in 1892, by combining the Thomson-Houston and the Edison. To his continued service, supported by other Thomson-Houston men in high positions, the great prosperity of the company is, in large part, due. The two companies so combined controlled probably one-half of all electrical patents then existing in America; and certainly more than half of those which had any considerable value.

In 1896 the General Electric pooled its patents with the Westinghouse, and thus competition was further restricted. In 1903 the General Electric absorbed the Stanley Electric Company, its other large competitor; and became the largest manufacturer of electric apparatus and machinery in the world. In 1912 the resources of the Company were $131,942,144. It billed sales to the amount of $89,182,185. It employed directly over 60,000 persons—more than a fourth as many as the Steel Trust. And it is protected against "undue" competition; for one of the Morgan partners has been a director, since 1909, in the Westinghouse—the only other large electrical machinery company in America.

The Automobile

The automobile industry is about twenty years old. It is now America's most prosperous business. When Henry B. Joy, President of the Packard Motor Car Company, was asked to what extent the bankers aided in "initiating" the automobile, he replied:

> It is the observable facts of history, it is also my experience of thirty years as a business man, banker, etc., that first the seer conceives an opportunity. He has faith in his almost second sight. He believes he can do something—develop a business—construct an industry—build a railroad—or Niagara Falls Power Company—and make it pay!
> Now the human measure is not the actual physical construction, but the "make it pay"!

A man raised the money in the late '90s and built a beet sugar factory in Michigan. Wiseacres said it was nonsense. He gathered together the money from his friends who would take a chance with him. He not only built the sugar factory (and there was never any doubt of his ability to do that) but he made it pay. The next year two more sugar factories were built, and were financially successful. These were built by private individuals of wealth, taking chances in the face of cries of doubting bankers and trust companies.

Once demonstrated that the industry was a sound one financially and *then* bankers and trust companies would lend the new sugar companies which were speedily organized a large part of the necessary funds to construct and operate.

The motor-car business was the same.

When a few gentlemen followed me in my vision of the possibilities of the business, the banks and older business men (who in the main were the banks) said, "fools and their money soon to be parted"—etc., etc.

Private capital at first establishes an industry, backs it through its troubles, and, if possible, wins financial success when banks would not lend a dollar of aid.

The business once having proved to be practicable and financially successful, then do the banks lend aid to its needs.

Such also was the experience of the greatest of the many financial successes in the automobile industry—the Ford Motor Company.

How Bankers Arrest Development

But "great banking houses" have not merely failed to initiate industrial development; they have definitely arrested development because to them the creation of the trusts is largely due. The recital in the Memorial addressed to the President by the Investors' Guild in November, 1911, is significant:

> It is a well-known fact that modern trade combinations tend strongly toward constancy of process and products, and by their very nature are opposed to new processes and new products originated by independent inventors, and hence tend to restrain competition in the development and sale of patents and patent rights; and consequently tend to discourage independent inventive thought, to the great detriment of the nation, and with injustice to inventors whom the Constitution especially intended to encourage and protect in their rights.

And more specific was the testimony of the *Engineering News:*

> We are today something like five years behind Germany in iron and steel metallurgy, and such innovations as are being introduced by our

iron and steel manufacturers are most of them merely following the lead set by foreigners years ago.

We do not believe this is because American engineers are any less ingenious or original than those of Europe, though they may indeed be deficient in training and scientific education compared with those of Germany. We believe the main cause is the wholesale consolidation which has taken place in American industry. A huge organization is too clumsy to take up the development of an original idea. With the market closely controlled and profits certain by following standard methods, those who control our trusts do not want the bother of developing anything new.

We instance metallurgy only by way of illustration. There are plenty of other fields of industry where exactly the same condition exists. We are building the same machines and using the same methods as a dozen years ago, and the real advances in the art are being made by European inventors and manufacturers.

To which President Wilson's statement may be added:

I am not saying that all invention had been stopped by the growth of trusts, but I think it is perfectly clear that invention in many fields has been discouraged, that inventors have been prevented from reaping the full fruits of their ingenuity and industry, and that mankind has been deprived of many comforts and conveniences, as well as the opportunity of buying at lower prices.

Do you know, have you had occasion to learn, that there is no hospitality for invention, now-a-days?

Trusts and Financial Concentration

The fact that industrial monopolies arrest development is more serious even than the direct burden imposed through extortionate prices. But the most harm-bearing incident of the trusts is their promotion of financial concentration. Industrial trusts feed the money trust. Practically every trust created has destroyed the financial independence of some communities and of many properties; for it has centered the financing of a large part of whole lines of business in New York, and this usually with one of a few banking houses. This is well illustrated by the Steel Trust, which is a trust of trusts; that is, the Steel Trust combines in one huge holding company the trusts previously formed in the different branches of the steel business. Thus the Tube Trust combined 17 tube mills, located in 16 different cities, scattered over 5 states and owned by 13 different companies. The wire trust combined 19 mills; the sheet steel trust 26; the bridge and structural trust 27; and the tin plate trust 36; all scattered similarly over many states. Finally these and other companies were formed into the United States Steel Corporation, combining 228 companies in all, located in 127 cities and towns, scattered over 18 states. Before the combinations were effected, nearly every one of these companies was owned largely by those who managed it, and had been financed, to a large extent, in the place, or in the state, in which it was located. When the Steel Trust was formed all these concerns came under one management. Thereafter, the financing of each of these 228 corporations (and some which were later acquired) had to be done through or with the consent of J. P. Morgan & Co. *That was the greatest step in financial concentration ever taken.*

Stock Exchange Incidents

The organization of trusts has served in another way to increase the power of the Money Trust. Few of the independent concerns out of which the trusts have been formed, were listed on the New York Stock Exchange; and few of them had financial offices in New York. Promoters of large corporations, whose stock is to be held by the public, and also investors, desire to have their securities listed on the New York Stock Exchange. Under the rules of the Exchange, no security can be so listed unless the corporation has a transfer agent and registrar in New York City. Furthermore, banker-directorships have contributed largely to the establishment of the financial offices of the trusts in New York City. That alone would tend to financial concentration. But the listing of the stock enhances the power of the Money Trust in another way. An industrial stock, once listed, frequently becomes the subject of active speculation; and speculation feeds the Money Trust indirectly in many ways. It draws the money of the country to New York. The New York bankers handle the loans of other people's money on the Stock Exchange; and members of the Stock Exchange receive large amounts from commissions. For instance: There are 5,084,952 shares of United States Steel common stock outstanding. But in the five years ending December 31, 1912, speculation in that stock was so extensive that there were sold on the Exchange an average of 29,380,888 shares a year; or nearly six times as much as there is Steel common in existence. Except where the transactions are by or for the brokers, sales on the Exchange involve the payment of twenty-five cents in commission for each share of stock sold; that is, twelve and one-half cents by the seller and twelve and one-half cents by the buyer. Thus the commission from the Steel common alone afforded a revenue averaging many millions a year. The Steel preferred stock is also much traded in; and there are 138 other industrials, largely trusts, listed on the New York Stock Exchange.

Trust Ramifications

But the potency of trusts as a factor in financial concentration is manifested in still other ways; notably through their ramifying operations. This is illustrated forcibly by the General Electric Company's control of water-power companies which has now been disclosed in an able report of the United States Bureau of Corporations:

> The extent of the General Electric influence is not fully revealed by its consolidated balance sheet. A very large number of corporations are connected with it through its subsidiaries and through corporations controlled by these subsidiaries or affiliated with them. There is a still wider circle of influence due to the fact that officers and directors of the General Electric Co. and its subsidiaries are also officers or directors of many other corporations, some of whose securities are owned by the General Electric Company.
>
> The General Electric Company holds in the first place all the common stock in three security holding companies: the United Electric Securities Co., the Electrical Securities Corporation, and the Electric Bond and Share Co. Directly and through these corporations and their officers the General Electric controls a large part of the water power of the United States.
>
> . . . The water-power companies in the General Electric group are found in 18 States. These 18 States have 2,325,757 commercial horsepower [h.p.] developed or under construction, and of this total the General Electric group includes 939,115 h.p. or 40.4 per cent. The greatest amount of power controlled by the companies in the General Electric group in any State is found in Washington. This is followed by New York, Pennsylvania, California, Montana, Iowa, Oregon, and Colorado. In five of the States shown in the table the water-power companies included in the General Electric group control more than 50 per cent. of the commercial power, developed and under construction. The percentage of power in the States included in the General Electric group ranges from a little less than 2 per cent. in Michigan to nearly 80 per cent. in Pennsylvania. In Colorado they control 72 per cent.; in New Hampshire 61 per cent.; in Oregon 58 per cent.; and in Washington 55 per cent.
>
> Besides the power developed and under construction water-power concerns included in the General Electric group own in the States shown in the table 641,600 h.p. undeveloped.

This water power control enables the General Electric group to control other public service corporations:

The water-power companies subject to General Electric influence control the street railways in at least 16 cities and towns; the electric-light plants in 78 cities and towns; gas plants in 19 cities and towns; and are affiliated with the electric light and gas plants in other towns. Though many of these communities, particularly those served with light only, are small, several of them are the most important in the States where these water-power companies operate. The water-power companies in the General Electric group own, control, or are closely affiliated with, the street railways in Portland and Salem, Ore.; Spokane, Wash.; Great Falls, Mont.; St. Louis, Mo.; Winona, Minn.; Milwaukee and Racine, Wis.; Elmira, N.Y.; Asheville and Raleigh, N.C., and other relatively less important towns. The towns in which the lighting plants (electric or gas) are owned or controlled include Portland, Salem, Astoria, and other towns in Oregon; Bellingham and other towns in Washington; Butte, Great Falls, Bozeman, and other towns in Montana; Leadville and Colorado Springs in Colorado; St. Louis, Mo.; Milwaukee, Racine, and several small towns in Wisconsin; Hudson and Rensselaer, N.Y.; Detroit, Mich.; Asheville and Raleigh, N.C.; and in fact one or more towns in practically every community where developed water power is controlled by this group. In addition to the public-service corporations thus controlled by the water-power companies subject to General Electric influence, there are numerous public-service corporations in other municipalities that purchase power from the hydroelectric developments controlled by or affiliated with the General Electric Co. This is true of Denver, Colo., which has already been discussed. In Baltimore, Md., a water-power concern in the General Electric group, namely, the Pennsylvania Water & Power Co., sells 20,000 h.p. to the Consolidated Gas, Electric Light & Power Co., which controls the entire light and power business of that city. The power to operate all the electric street railway systems of Buffalo, N.Y., and vicinity, involving a trackage of approximately 375 miles, is supplied through a subsidiary of the Niagara Falls Power Co.

And the General Electric Company, through the financing of public service companies, exercises a like influence in communities where there is no water power:

It, or its subsidiaries, has acquired control of or an interest in the public-service corporations of numerous cities where there is no water-power connection, and it is affiliated with still others by virtue of common directors. . . . This vast network of relationship between hydro-electric corporations through prominent officers and directors of the largest manufacturer of electrical machinery and supplies in the United States is highly significant. . . .

It is possible that this relationship to such a large number of strong financial concerns, through common officers and directors, affords the General Electric Co. an advantage that may place rivals at a corresponding disadvantage. Whether or not this great financial power has been used to the particular disadvantage of any rival water-power concern is not so important as the fact that such power exists and that it might be so used at any time.

The Sherman Law

The Money Trust cannot be broken, if we allow its power to be constantly augmented. To break the Money Trust, we must stop that power at its source. The industrial trusts are among its most effective feeders. Those which are illegal should be dissolved. The creation of new ones should be prevented. To this end the Sherman Law should be supplemented both by providing more efficient judicial machinery, and by creating a commission with administrative functions to aid in enforcing the law. When that is done, another step will have been taken toward securing the New Freedom. But restrictive legislation alone will not suffice. We should bear in mind the admonition with which the Commissioner of Corporations closes his review of our water power development:

> There is . . . presented such a situation in water powers and other public utilities as might bring about at any time under a single management the control of a majority of the developed water power in the United States and similar control over the public utilities in a vast number of cities and towns, including some of the most important in the country.

We should conserve all rights which the Federal Government and the States now have in our natural resources, and there should be a complete separation of our industries from railroads and public utilities.

Chapter VIII

A Curse of Bigness

Bigness has been an important factor in the rise of the Money Trust: Big railroad systems, Big industrial trusts, Big public service companies; and as instruments of these Big banks and Big trust companies. J. P. Morgan & Co. (in their letter of defense to the Pujo Committee) urge the needs of

Big Business as the justification for financial concentration. They declare that what they euphemistically call "cooperation" is "simply a further result of the necessity for handling great transactions"; that "the country obviously requires not only the larger individual banks, but demands also that those banks shall cooperate to perform efficiently the country's business"; and that "a step backward along this line would mean a halt in industrial progress that would affect every wage-earner from the Atlantic to the Pacific." The phrase "great transactions" is used by the bankers apparently as meaning large corporate security issues.

Leading bankers have undoubtedly cooperated during the last 15 years in floating some very large security issues, as well as many small ones. But relatively few large issues were made necessary by great improvements undertaken or by industrial development. Improvements and development ordinarily proceed slowly. For them, even where the enterprise involves large expenditures, a series of small issues is usually more appropriate than single large ones. This is particularly true in the East where the building of new railroads has practically ceased. The "great" security issues in which bankers have cooperated were, with relatively few exceptions, made either for the purpose of effecting combinations or as a consequence of such combinations. Furthermore, the combinations which made necessary these large security issues or underwritings were, in most cases, either contrary to existing statute law, or contrary to laws recommended by the Interstate Commerce Commission, or contrary to the laws of business efficiency. So both the financial concentration and the combinations which they have served were, in the main, against the public interest. Size, we are told, is not a crime. But size may, at least, become noxious by reason of the means through which it was attained or the uses to which it is put. And it is size attained by combination, instead of natural growth, which has contributed so largely to our financial concentration. Let us examine a few cases:

The Harriman Pacifics

J. P. Morgan & Co., in urging the "need of large banks and the cooperation of bankers," said: "The Attorney-General's recent approval of the Union Pacific settlement calls for a single commitment on the part of bankers of $126,000,000."

This $126,000,000 "commitment" was not made to enable the Union Pacific to secure capital. On the contrary it was a guaranty that it would succeed in disposing of its Southern Pacific stock to that amount. And when it had disposed of that stock, it was confronted with the serious problem—what to do with the proceeds? This huge underwriting became necessary solely because the Union Pacific had violated the Sherman Law. It had acquired that amount of Southern Pacific stock illegally; and the Supreme Court of the United States finally decreed that the illegality cease. This same illegal purchase had been the occasion, twelve years earlier, of another "great transaction"—the issue of $100,000,000 of Union Pacific bonds, which were sold to provide funds for acquiring this Southern Pacific and other stocks in violation of law. Bankers "cooperated" also to accomplish that.

Union Pacific Improvements

The Union Pacific and its auxiliary lines (the Oregon Short Line, the Oregon Railway and Navigation, and the Oregon-Washington Railroad) made, in the fourteen years, ending June 30, 1912, issues of securities aggregating $375,158,183 (of which $46,500,000 were refunded or redeemed*); but the large security issues served mainly to supply funds for engaging in illegal combinations or stock speculation. The extraordinary improvements and additions that raised the Union Pacific Railroad to a high state of efficiency were provided mainly by the net earnings from the operation of its railroads. And note how great the improvements and additions were: Tracks were straightened, grades were lowered, bridges were rebuilt, heavy rails were laid, old equipment was replaced by new; and the cost of these was charged largely as operating expense. Additional equipment was added, new lines were built or acquired, increasing the system by 3524 miles of line, and still other improvements and betterments were made and charged to capital account. These expenditures aggregated $191,512,328. But it needed no "large security issues" to provide the capital thus wisely expended. The net earnings from the operations of these railroads were so large that nearly all these improvements and additions could have been made without issuing on the average more than $1,000,000 a year of additional securities for "new money," and the company still could have paid six per cent. dividends after 1906 (when that rate was adopted). For while $13,679,452 a year, on the average, was charged to Cost of Road and Equipment, the surplus net earnings and other funds would have yielded, on the average, $12,750,982 a year available for improvements and additions, without raising money on new security issues.

---

* A bond or other form of commercial loan is said to be *redeemed* when the holder is paid both principal and interest in full; it is *refunded* when in place of the old security, the holder gets a new bond whose face value is equal to the principal and the unpaid, accrued interest.

How the Security Proceeds Were Spent

The $375,000,000 securities (except to the extent of about $13,000,000 required for improvements, and the amounts applied for refunding and redemptions) were available to buy stocks and bonds of other companies. And some of the stocks so acquired were sold at large profits, providing further sums to be employed in stock purchases.

The $375,000,000 Union Pacific Lines security issues, therefore, were not needed to supply funds for Union Pacific improvements; nor did these issues supply funds for the improvement of any of the companies in which the Union Pacific invested (except that certain amounts were advanced later to aid in financing the Southern Pacific). *They served, substantially, no purpose save to transfer the ownership of railroad stocks from one set of persons to another.*

Here are some of the principal investments:

1. $91,657,500, in acquiring and financing the Southern Pacific.
2. $89,391,401, in acquiring the Northern Pacific stock and stock of the Northern Securities Co.
3. $45,466,960, in acquiring Baltimore & Ohio stock.
4. $37,692,256, in acquiring Illinois Central stock.
5. $23,205,679, in acquiring New York Central stock.
6. $10,395,000, in acquiring Atchison, Topeka & Santa Fe stock.
7. $8,946,781, in acquiring Chicago & Alton stock.
8. $11,610,187, in acquiring Chicago, Milwaukee & St. Paul stock.
9. $6,750,423, in acquiring Chicago & Northwestern stock.
10. $6,936,696, in acquiring Railroad Securities Co. stock (Illinois Central stock).

The immediate effect of these stock acquisitions, as stated by the Interstate Commerce Commission in 1907, was merely this:

Mr. Harriman may journey by steamship from New York to New Orleans, thence by rail to San Francisco, across the Pacific Ocean to China, and, returning by another route to the United States, may go to Ogden by any one of three rail lines, and thence to Kansas City or Omaha, without leaving the deck or platform of a carrier which he controls, and without duplicating any part of his journey.

He has further what appears to be a dominant control in the Illinois Central Railroad running directly north from the Gulf of Mexico to the Great Lakes, parallel to the Mississippi River; and two thousand miles west of the Mississippi he controls the only line of railroad parallel to the Pacific Coast, and running from the Colorado River to the Mexican border. . . .

The testimony taken at this hearing shows that about fifty thousand square miles of territory in the State of Oregon, surrounded by the lines of the Oregon Short Line Railroad Company, the Oregon Railroad and Navigation Company, and the Southern Pacific Company, is not developed. While the funds of those companies which could be used for that purpose are being invested in stocks like the New York Central and other lines having only a remote relation to the territory in which the Union Pacific System is located.

Mr. Harriman succeeded in becoming director in 27 railroads with 39,354 miles of line; and they extended from the Atlantic to the Pacific; from the Great Lakes to the Gulf of Mexico.

The Aftermath

On September 9, 1909, less than twelve years after Mr. Harriman first became a director in the Union Pacific, he died from overwork at the age of 61. But it was not death only that had set a limit to his achievements. The multiplicity of his interests prevented him from performing for his other railroads the great services that had won him a world-wide reputation as manager and rehabilitator of the Union Pacific and the Southern Pacific. Within a few months after Mr. Harriman's death the serious equipment scandal* on the Illinois Central became public, culminating in the probable suicide of one of the vice-presidents of that company. The Chicago & Alton (in the management of which Mr. Harriman was prominent from 1899 to 1907, as President, Chairman of the Board, or Executive Committeeman), has never regained the prosperity it enjoyed before he and his associates acquired control. The Père Marquette has passed again into receiver's** hands. Long before Mr. Harriman's death the Union Pacific had disposed of its Northern Pacific stock, because the Supreme Court of the United States declared the Northern Securities Company illegal, and dissolved the Northern Pacific–Great Northern merger. Three years after his death, the Supreme Court of the United States ordered the Union Pacific–Southern Pacific merger dissolved. By a strange irony, the law has permitted the Union Pacific to reap large profits from its illegal transactions in Northern Pacific and Southern Pacific stocks. But many other stocks held "as investments" have entailed large losses. Stocks in the Illinois Central and other companies which cost the Union Pacific $129,894,991.72, had on

---

*Harriman spent so much money on expanding his holdings that he failed to maintain and replace worn-out equipment, a fact that became clear after his death.

**When a company is forced into bankruptcy, a judge will appoint a *receiver*, a supposedly independent outsider who will run the affairs of the firm until either it is reorganized and put back on a sound financial footing or it is closed down and its assets are sold off to pay the creditors.

November 15, 1913, a market value of only $87,851,500; showing a shrinkage of $42,043,491.72 and the average income from them, while held, was only about 4.30 per cent. on their cost.

A Bankers' Paradise

Kuhn, Loeb & Co. were the Union Pacific bankers. It was in pursuance of a promise which Mr. Jacob H. Schiff—the senior partner—had given, pending the reorganization, that Mr. Harriman first became a member of the Executive Committee in 1897. Thereafter combinations grew and crumbled, and there were vicissitudes in stock speculations. But the investment bankers prospered amazingly; and financial concentration proceeded without abatement. The bankers and their associates received the commissions paid for purchasing the stocks which the Supreme Court holds to have been acquired illegally—and have retained them. The bankers received commissions for underwriting the securities issued to raise the money with which to buy the stocks which the Supreme Court holds to have been illegally acquired, and have retained them. The bankers received commissions paid for floating securities of the controlled companies—while they were thus controlled in violation of law—and have, of course, retained them. Finally when, after years, a decree is entered to end the illegal combination, these same bankers are on hand to perform the services of undertaker—and receive further commissions for their banker-aid in enabling the law-breaking corporation to end its wrong doing and to comply with the decree of the Supreme Court. And yet, throughout nearly all this long period, both before and after Mr. Harriman's death, two partners in Kuhn, Loeb & Co. were directors or members of the executive committee of the Union Pacific; and as such must be deemed responsible with others for the illegal acts.

Indeed, these bankers have not only received commissions for the underwritings of transactions accomplished, though illegal; they have received commissions also for merely *agreeing* to underwrite a "great transaction" which the authorities would not permit to be *accomplished.* The $126,000,000 underwriting (that "single commitment on the part of bankers" to which J. P. Morgan & Co. refer as being called for by "the Attorney General's approval of the Union Pacific settlement") never became effective; because the Public Service Commission of California refused to approve the terms of settlement. But the Union Pacific, nevertheless, paid the Kuhn Loeb Syndicate a large underwriting fee for having been ready and willing "to serve," should the opportunity arise: and another underwriting commission was paid when the Southern Pacific stock was finally distributed, with the approval of Attorney General McReynolds, under the Court's decree. Thus the illegal purchase of Southern Pacific stock yielded directly four crops of commissions; two when it was acquired, and two when it was disposed of. And during the intervening period the illegally controlled Southern Pacific yielded many more commissions to the bankers. For the schedules filed with the Pujo Committee show that Kuhn, Loeb & Co. marketed, in addition to the Union Pacific securities above referred to, $334,000,000 of Southern Pacific and Central Pacific securities between 1903 and 1911.

The aggregate amount of the commissions paid to these bankers in connection with Union Pacific–Southern Pacific transactions is not disclosed. It must have been very large; for not only were the transactions "great"; but the commissions were liberal. The Interstate Commerce Commission finds that bankers received about 5 per cent. on the purchase price for buying the first 750,000 shares of Southern Pacific stock; and the underwriting commission on the first $100,000,000 Union Pacific bonds issued to make that and other purchases was $5,000,000. How large the two underwriting commissions were which the Union Pacific paid in effecting the severance of this illegal merger, both the company and the bankers have declined to disclose. Furthermore the Interstate Commerce Commission showed, clearly, while investigating the Union Pacific's purchase of the Chicago & Alton stock, that the bankers' profits were by no means confined to commissions.

The Burlington

Such railroad combinations produce injury to the public far more serious than the heavy tax of bankers' commissions and profits. For in nearly every case the absorption into a great system of a theretofore independent railroad has involved the loss of financial independence to some community, property, or men, who thereby become subjects or satellites of the Money Trust. The passing of the Chicago, Burlington & Quincy, in 1901, to the Morgan associates, presents a striking example of this process.

After the Union Pacific acquired the Southern Pacific stock in 1901, it sought control, also, of the Chicago, Burlington & Quincy—a most prosperous railroad, having then 7912 miles of line. The Great Northern and Northern Pacific recognized that Union Pacific control of the Burlington would exclude them from much of Illinois, Missouri, Wisconsin, Kansas, Nebraska, Iowa, and South Dakota. The two northern roads, which were already closely allied with each other and with J. P. Morgan & Co., thereupon purchased for $215,227,000, of their joint 4 per cent. bonds, nearly all of the $109,324,000 (par value) outstanding Burlington stock. A struggle with the Union Pacific ensued which yielded soon to "harmonious cooperation." The Northern Securities Company was formed with $400,000,000 capital, thereby merging the Great Northern, the Northern Pacific, and the Burlington, and joining the Harriman, Kuhn-Loeb, with the Morgan-Hill interests. Obviously neither the issue of $215,000,000 joint 4's, nor the issue of the $400,000,000 Northern Securities stock supplied one dollar of funds for improvements of, or additions to, any of the four great railroad systems concerned in these "large transactions." *The sole effect of issuing $615,000,000 of securities was to transfer stock from one set of persons to another.* And the resulting "harmonious cooperation" was soon interrupted by the government proceedings, which ended with the dissolution of the Northern Securities Company. But the evil done outlived the combination. The Burlington had passed forever from its independent Boston owners to the Morgan allies, who remain in control.

The Burlington — one of Boston's finest achievements — was the creation of John M. Forbes. He was a builder; not a combiner, or banker, or wizard of finance. He was a simple, hard-working business man. He had been a merchant in China at a time when China's trade was among America's big business. He had been connected with shipping and with manufactures. He had the imagination of the great merchant; the patience and perseverance of the great manufacturer; the courage of the sea-farer; and the broad view of the statesman. Bold, but never reckless; scrupulously careful of other people's money, he was ready, after due weighing of chances, to risk his own in enterprises promising success. He was in the best sense of the term, a great adventurer. Thus equipped, Mr. Forbes entered, in 1852, upon those railroad enterprises which later developed into the Chicago, Burlington & Quincy. Largely with his own money and that of friends who confided in him, he built these railroads and carried them through the panic of '57, when the "great banking houses" of those days lacked courage to assume the burdens of a struggling ill-constructed line, staggering under financial difficulties.

Under his wise management, and that of the men whom he trained, the little Burlington became a great system. It was "built on honor," and managed honorably. It weathered every other great financial crisis, as it did that of 1857. It reached maturity without a reorganization or the sacrifice of a single stockholder or bondholder.

Investment bankers had no place on the Burlington Board of Directors; nor had the banker-practice, of being on both sides of a bargain. "I am unwilling," said Mr. Forbes, early in his career, "to run the risk of having the imputation of buying from a company in which I am interested." About twenty years later he made his greatest fight to rescue the Burlington from the control of certain contractor-directors, whom his biographer, Mr. Pearson, describes as "persons of integrity, who had conceived that in their twofold capacity as contractors and directors they were fully able to deal with themselves justly." Mr. Forbes thought otherwise. The stockholders, whom he had aroused, sided with him and he won.

Mr. Forbes was the pioneer among Boston railroad-builders. His example and his success inspired many others, for Boston was not lacking then in men who were builders, though some lacked his wisdom, and some his character. Her enterprise and capital constructed, in large part, the Union Pacific, the Atchison, the Mexican Central, the Wisconsin Central, and 24 other railroads in the West and South. One by one these western and southern railroads passed out of Boston control; the greater part of them into the control of the Morgan allies. Before the Burlington was surrendered, Boston had begun to lose her dominion, even, over the railroads of New England. In 1900 the Boston & Albany was leased to the New York Central—a Morgan property; and a few years later, another Morgan railroad—the New Haven—acquired control of nearly every other transportation line in New England. Now nothing is left of Boston's railroad dominion in the West and South, except the Eastern Kentucky Railroad—a line 36 miles long; and her control of the railroads of Massachusetts is limited to the Grafton & Upton with 19 miles of line and the Boston, Revere Beach & Lynn—a passenger road 13 miles long.

The New Haven Monopoly

The rise of the New Haven Monopoly presents another striking example of combination as a developer of financial concentration; and it illustrates also the use to which "large security issues" are put.

In 1892, when Mr. Morgan entered the New Haven directorate, it was a very prosperous little railroad with capital liabilities of $25,000,000 paying 10 per cent. dividends, and operating 508 miles of line. By 1899 the capitalization had grown to $80,477,600, but the aggregate mileage had also grown (mainly through merger or leases of other lines) to 2017. Fourteen years later, in 1913, when Mr. Morgan died and Mr. Mellen* resigned, the mileage was 1997, just 20 miles less than in 1899; but the capital liabilities had increased to $425,935,000. Of course the business of the railroad had grown largely in those fourteen years; the road-bed was improved, bridges built, additional tracks added, and much equipment

---

* *Charles S. Mellen* had started as a railway clerk and had risen to become J. P. Morgan's lieutenant as president of the New Haven Railroad. Mellen worked assiduously to merge the New Haven with other lines and to secure a monopoly of New England transportation.

purchased; and for all this, new capital was needed; and additional issues were needed, also, because the company paid out in dividends more than it earned. But of the capital increase, over $200,000,000 was expended in the acquisition of the stock or other securities of some 121 other railroads, steamships, street railway-, electric-light-, gas-, and water-companies. It was these outside properties, which made necessary the much discussed $67,000,000, 6 per cent. bond issue, as well as other large and expensive security issues. For in these fourteen years the improvements on the railroad including new equipment have cost, on the average, only $10,000,000 a year.

The New Haven Bankers

Few, if any, of those 121 companies which the New Haven acquired had, prior to their absorption by it, been financed by J. P. Morgan & Co. The needs of the Boston & Maine and Maine Central—the largest group—had, for generations, been met mainly through their own stockholders or through Boston banking houses. No investment banker had been a member of the Board of Directors of either of those companies. The New York, Ontario & Western—the next largest of the acquired railroads—had been financed in New York, but by persons apparently entirely independent of the Morgan allies. The smaller Connecticut railroads, now combined in the Central New England, had been financed mainly in Connecticut, or by independent New York bankers. The financing of the street railway companies had been done largely by individual financiers, or by small and independent bankers in the states or cities where the companies operate. Some of the steamship companies had been financed by their owners, some through independent bankers. As the result of the absorption of these 121 companies into the New Haven system, the financing of all these railroads, steamship companies, street railways, and other corporations, was made tributary to J. P. Morgan & Co.; and the independent bankers were eliminated or became satellites. *And this financial concentration was proceeded with, although practically every one of these 121 companies was acquired by the New Haven in violation either of the state or federal law, or of both.* Enforcement of the Sherman Act will doubtless result in dissolving this unwieldy illegal combination.

The Coal Monopoly

Proof of the "cooperation" of the anthracite railroads is furnished by the ubiquitous presence of George F. Baker on the Board of Directors of the Reading, the Jersey Central, the Lackawanna, the Lehigh, the Erie, and the New York, Susquehanna & Western railroads, which together control nearly all the unmined anthracite as well as the actual tonnage. These roads have been an important factor in the development of the Money Trust. They are charged by the Department of Justice with fundamental violations both of the Sherman Law and of the Commodity clause of the Hepburn Act, which prohibits a railroad from carrying, in interstate trade, any commodity in which it has an interest, direct or indirect. Nearly every large issue of securities made in the last 14 years by any of these railroads (except the Erie), has been in connection with some act of combination. The combination of the anthracite railroads to suppress the construction, through the Temple Iron Company, of a competing coal road, has already been declared illegal by the Supreme Court of the United States. And in the bituminous coal field—the Kanawha District—the United States Circuit Court of Appeals has recently decreed that a similar combination by the Lake Shore, the Chesapeake & Ohio, and the Hocking Valley, be dissolved.

Other Railroad Combinations

The cases of the Union Pacific and of the New Haven are typical—not exceptional. Our railroad history presents numerous instances of large security issues made wholly or mainly to effect combinations. Some of these combinations have been proper as a means of securing natural feeders or extensions of main lines. But far more of them have been dictated by the desire to suppress active or potential competition; or by personal ambition or greed; or by the mistaken belief that efficiency grows with size.

Thus the monstrous combination of the Rock Island and the St. Louis and San Francisco with over 14,000 miles of line is recognized now to have been obviously inefficient. It was severed voluntarily; but, had it not been, must have crumbled soon from inherent defects, if not as a result of proceedings under the Sherman law. Both systems are suffering now from the effects of this unwise combination; the Frisco, itself greatly over-combined, has paid the penalty in receivership. The Rock Island—a name once expressive of railroad efficiency and stability—has, through its excessive recapitalizations and combinations, become a football of speculators, and a source of great apprehension to confiding investors. The combination of the Cincinnati, Hamilton and Dayton, and the Père Marquette led to several receiverships.

There are, of course, other combinations which have not been disastrous to the owners of the railroads. But the fact that a railroad combination has not been disastrous does not necessarily justify it. The evil of the concentration of power is obvious; and as combination necessarily involves such concentration of power, the burden of justifying a combination should be placed upon those who seek to effect it.

For instance, what public good has been subserved by allowing the Atlantic Coast Line Railroad Company to issue $50,000,000 of securities to acquire control of the Louisville & Nashville Railroad—a widely extended, self-sufficient system of 5000 miles, which, under the wise management of President Milton H. Smith had prospered continuously for many years before the acquisition; and which has gross earnings nearly twice as large as those of the Atlantic Coast Line. The legality of this combination has been recently challenged by Senator Lea;* and an investigation by the Interstate Commerce Commission has been ordered.

The Pennsylvania

The reports from the Pennsylvania suggest the inquiry whether even this generally well-managed railroad is not suffering from excessive bigness. After 1898 it, too, bought, in large amounts, stocks in other railroads, including the Chesapeake & Ohio, the Baltimore & Ohio, and the Norfolk & Western. In 1906 it sold all its Chesapeake & Ohio stock, and a majority of its Baltimore & Ohio and Norfolk & Western holdings. Later it reversed its policy and resumed stock purchases, acquiring, among others, more Norfolk & Western and New York, New Haven & Hartford; and on Dec. 31, 1912, held securities valued at $331,909,154.32; of which, however, a large part represents Pennsylvania System securities. These securities (mostly stocks) constitute about one-third of the total assets of the Pennsylvania Railroad. The income on these securities in 1912 averaged only 4.30 per cent. on their valuation, while the Pennsylvania paid 6 per cent. on its stock. But the cost of carrying these foreign stocks is not limited to the difference between this income and outgo. To raise money on these stocks the Pennsylvania had to issue its own securities; and there is such a thing as an over-supply even of Pennsylvania securities. Over-supply of any stock depresses market values, and increases the cost to the Pennsylvania of raising new money. Recently came the welcome announcement of the management that it will dispose of its stocks in the anthracite coal mines; and it is intimated that it will divest itself also of other holdings in companies (like the Cambria Steel Company) extraneous to the business of railroading. This policy should be extended to include the disposition also

---

Luke Lea represented Wisconsin in the United States Senate.

of all stock in other railroads (like the Norfolk & Western, the Southern Pacific, and the New Haven) which are not a part of the Pennsylvania System.

Recommendations

Six years ago the Interstate Commerce Commission, after investigating the Union Pacific transaction above referred to, recommended legislation to remedy the evils there disclosed. Upon concluding recently its investigation of the New Haven, the Commission repeated and amplified those recommendations, saying:

> No student of the railroad problem can doubt that a most prolific source of financial disaster and complication to railroads in the past has been the desire and ability of railroad managers to engage in enterprises outside the legitimate operation of their railroads, especially by the acquisition of other railroads and their securities. The evil which results, first, to the investing public, and, finally, to the general public, cannot be corrected after the transaction has taken place; it can be easily and effectively prohibited. In our opinion the following propositions lie at the foundation of all adequate regulation of interstate railroads:
>
> 1. Every interstate railroad should be prohibited from spending money or incurring liability or acquiring property not in the operation of its railroad or in the legitimate improvement, extension, or development of that railroad.
> 2. No interstate railroad should be permitted to lease or purchase any other railroad, nor to acquire the stocks or securities of any other railroad, nor to guarantee the same, directly or indirectly, without the approval of the federal government.
> 3. No stocks or bonds should be issued by an interstate railroad except for the purposes sanctioned in the two preceding paragraphs, and none should be issued without the approval of the federal government.
>
> It may be unwise to attempt to specify the price at which and the manner in which railroad stocks and securities shall be disposed of; but it is easy and safe to define the purpose for which they may be issued and to confine the expenditure of the money realized to that purpose.

These recommendations are in substantial accord with those adopted by the National Association of Railway Commissioners. They should be enacted into law. And they should be supplemented by amendments of the Commodity Clause of the Hepburn Act, so that:

1. Railroads will be effectually prohibited from owning stock in corporations whose products they transport;
2. Such corporations will be prohibited from owning important stockholdings in railroads; and
3. Holding companies will be prohibited from controlling, as does the Reading, both a railroad and corporations whose commodities it transports.

If laws such as these are enacted and duly enforced, we shall be protected from a recurrence of tragedies like the New Haven, of domestic scandals like the Chicago and Alton, and of international ones like the Frisco. We shall also escape from that inefficiency which is attendant upon excessive size. But what is far more important, we shall, by such legislation, remove a potent factor in financial concentration. Decentralization will begin. The liberated smaller units will find no difficulty in financing their needs without bowing the knee to money lords. And a long step will have been taken toward attainment of the New Freedom.

Chapter IX

The Failure of Banker-Management

There is not one moral, but many, to be drawn from the Decline of the New Haven and the Fall of Mellen. That history offers texts for many sermons. It illustrates the Evils of Monopoly, the Curse of Bigness, the Futility of Lying, and the Pitfalls of Law-Breaking. But perhaps the most impressive lesson that it should teach to investors is the failure of banker-management.

Banker Control

For years J. P. Morgan & Co. were the fiscal agents of the New Haven. For years Mr. Morgan was *the* director of the Company. He gave to that property probably closer personal attention than to any other of his many interests. Stockholders' meetings are rarely interesting or important; and few indeed must have been the occasions when Mr. Morgan attended any stockholders' meeting of other companies in which he was a director. But it was his habit, when in America, to be present at meetings of the New Haven. In 1907, when the policy of monopolistic expansion was first challenged, and again at the meeting in 1909 (after Massachusetts had unwisely accorded its sanction to the Boston & Maine merger), Mr. Morgan himself moved the large increases of stock which were unanimously voted. Of course, he attended the important directors' meetings. His will was law. President Mellen indicated this in his statement before Interstate Commerce Commissioner Prouty, while discussing the New York, Westchester & Boston—the railroad without a terminal in New York, which cost the New Haven $1,500,000 a mile to acquire, and was then costing it, in operating deficits and interest charges, $100,000 a month to run:

> I am in a very embarrassing position, Mr. Commissioner, regarding the New York, Westchester & Boston. I have never been enthusiastic or at all optimistic of its being a good investment for our company in the present, or in the immediate future; but people in whom I had greater confidence than I have in myself thought it was wise and desirable; I yielded my judgment; indeed, I don't know that it would have made much difference whether I yielded or not.

The Bankers' Responsibility

Bankers are credited with being a conservative force in the community. The tradition lingers that they are preeminently "safe and sane." And yet, the most grievous fault of this banker-managed railroad has been its financial recklessness—a fault that has already brought heavy losses to many thousands of small investors throughout New England for whom bankers are supposed to be natural guardians. In a community where its railroad stocks have for generations been deemed absolutely safe investments, the passing of the New Haven and of the Boston & Maine dividends after an unbroken dividend record of generations comes as a disaster.

This disaster is due mainly to enterprises outside the legitimate operation of these railroads; for no railroad company has equaled the New Haven in the quantity and extravagance of its outside enterprises. But it must be remembered, that neither the president of the New Haven nor any other railroad manager could engage in such transactions without the sanction of the Board of Directors. It is the directors, not Mr. Mellen, who should bear the responsibility.

Close scrutiny of the transactions discloses no justification. On the contrary, scrutiny serves only to make more clear the gravity of the errors committed. Not merely were recklessly extravagant acquisitions made in mad pursuit of monopoly; but the financial judgment, the financiering itself, was conspicuously bad. To pay for property several times what it is worth, to engage in grossly unwise enterprises, are errors of which no conservative directors should be found guilty; for perhaps the most important function of directors is to test the conclusions and curb by calm counsel the excessive zeal of too ambitious managers. But while we have no right to expect from bankers exceptionally good judgment in ordinary business matters; we do have a right to expect from them prudence, reasonably good financiering, and insistence upon straightforward accounting. And it is just the lack of these qualities in the New Haven management to which the severe criticism of the Interstate Commerce Commission is particularly directed.

Commissioner Prouty calls attention to the vast increase of capitalization. During the nine years beginning July 1, 1903, the capital of the New York, New Haven & Hartford Railroad Company itself increased from $93,000,000 to about $417,000,000 (excluding premiums). That fact alone would not convict the management of reckless financiering; but the fact that so little of the new capital was represented by stock might well raise a question as to its conservativeness. For the indebtedness (including guaranties) was increased over twenty times (from about $14,000,000 to $300,000,000), while the stock outstanding in the hands of the public was not doubled ($80,000,000 to $158,000,000). Still, in these days of large things, even such growth of corporate liabilities might be consistent with "safe and sane management."

But what can be said in defense of the financial judgment of the banker-management under which these two railroads find themselves confronted, in the fateful year 1913, with a most disquieting floating indebtedness? On March 31, the New Haven had outstanding $43,000,000 in short-time notes; the Boston & Maine had then outstanding $24,500,000, which have been increased since to $27,000,000; and additional notes have been issued by several of its subsidiary lines. Mainly to meet its share of these loans, the New Haven, which before its great expansion could sell at par 3½ per cent. bonds convertible into stock at $150 a share, was so eager to issue at par $67,500,000 of its 6 per cent. 20-year bonds convertible into stock as to agree to pay J. P. Morgan & Co. a 2½ per cent. underwriting commission. True, money was "tight" then. But is it not very bad financiering to be so unprepared for the "tight" money market which had been long expected? Indeed, the New Haven's management, particularly, ought to have avoided such an error; for it committed a similar one in the "tight" money market of

1907–1908, when it had to sell at par $39,000,000 of its 6 per cent. 40-year bonds.

These huge short-time borrowings of the System were not due to unexpected emergencies or to their monetary conditions. They were of gradual growth. On June 30, 1910, the two companies owed in short-term notes only $10,180,364; by June 30, 1911, the amount had grown to $30,759,959; by June 30, 1912, to $45,395,000; and in 1913 to over $70,000,000. Of course the rate of interest on the loans increased also very largely. And these loans were incurred unnecessarily. They represent, in the main, not improvements on the New Haven or on the Boston & Maine Railroads, but money borrowed either to pay for stocks in other companies which these companies could not afford to buy, or to pay dividends which had not been earned.

In five years out of the last six the New Haven Railroad has, on its own showing, paid dividends in excess of the year's earnings; and the annual deficits disclosed would have been much larger if proper charges for depreciation of equipment and of steamships had been made. In each of the last three years, during which the New Haven had absolute control of the Boston & Maine, the latter paid out in dividends so much in excess of earnings that before April, 1913, the surplus accumulated in earlier years had been converted into a deficit.

Surely these facts show, at least, an extraordinary lack of financial prudence.

Why Banker-Management Failed

Now, how can the failure of the banker-management of the New Haven be explained?

A few have questioned the ability; a few the integrity of the bankers. Commissioner Prouty attributed the mistakes made to the Company's pursuit of a transportation monopoly.

"The reason," says he, "is as apparent as the fact itself. The present management of that Company started out with the purpose of controlling the transportation facilities of New England. In the accomplishment of that purpose it bought what must be had and paid what must be paid. To this purpose and its attempted execution can be traced every one of these financial misfortunes and derelictions."

But it still remains to find the cause of the bad judgment exercised by the eminent banker-management in entering upon and in carrying out the policy of monopoly. For there were as grave errors in the execution of the policy of monopoly as in its adoption. Indeed, it was the aggregation of important errors of detail which compelled first the reduction, then the passing of dividends and which ultimately impaired the Company's credit. The failure of the banker-management of the New Haven cannot be explained as the shortcomings of individuals. The failure was not accidental. It was not exceptional. It was the natural result of confusing the functions of banker and business man.

Undivided Loyalty

The banker should be detached from the business for which he performs the banking service. This detachment is desirable, in the first place, in order to avoid conflict of interest. The relation of banker-directors to corporations which they finance has been a subject of just criticism. Their conflicting interests necessarily prevent single-minded devotion to the corporation. When a banker-director of a railroad decides as railroad man that it shall issue securities, and then sells them to himself as banker, fixing the price at which they are to be taken, there is necessarily grave danger that the interests of the railroad may suffer — suffer both through issuing of securities which ought not to be issued, and from selling them at a price less favorable to the company than should have been obtained. For it is ordinarily impossible for a banker-director to judge impartially between the corporation and himself. Even if he succeeded in being impartial, the relation would not conduce to the best interests of the company. The best bargains are made when buyer and seller are represented by different persons.

Detachment an Essential

But the objection to banker-management does not rest wholly, or perhaps mainly, upon the importance of avoiding divided loyalty. A complete detachment of the banker from the corporation is necessary in order to secure for the railroad the benefit of the clearest financial judgment; for the banker's judgment will be necessarily clouded by participation in the management or by ultimate responsibility for the policy actually pursued. It is *outside* financial advice which the railroad needs.

Long ago it was recognized that "a man who is his own lawyer has a fool for a client." The essential reason for this is that soundness of judgment is easily obscured by self-interest. Similarly, it is not the proper function of the banker to construct, purchase, or operate railroads, or to engage in industrial enterprises. The proper function of the banker is to give to or to withhold credit from other concerns; to purchase or to refuse to purchase securities from other concerns; and to sell securities to other customers. The proper exercise of this function demands that the banker should be wholly detached from the concern whose credit or securities are under consideration. His decision to grant or to withhold credit, to purchase or not to purchase securities, involves passing judgment on the efficiency of the management or the soundness of the enterprise; and he ought not to occupy a position where in doing so he is passing judgment on himself. Of course detachment does not imply lack of knowledge. The banker should act only with full knowledge, just as a lawyer should act only with full knowledge. The banker who undertakes to make loans to or purchase securities from a railroad for sale to his other customers ought to have as full knowledge of its affairs as does its legal adviser. But the banker should not be, in any sense, his own client. He should not, in the capacity of banker, pass judgment upon the wisdom of his own plans or acts as railroad man.

Such a detached attitude on the part of the banker is demanded also in the interest of his other customers—the purchasers of corporate securities. The investment banker stands toward a large part of his customers in a position of trust, which should be fully recognized. The small investors, particularly the women, who are holding an ever-increasing proportion of our corporate securities, commonly buy on the recommendation of their bankers. The small investors do not, and in most cases cannot, ascertain for themselves the facts on which to base a proper judgment as to the soundness of securities offered. And even if these investors were furnished with the facts, they lack the business experience essential to forming a proper judgment. Such investors need and are entitled to have the bankers' advice, and obviously their unbiased advice; and the advice cannot be unbiased where the banker, as part of the corporation's management, has participated in the creation of the securities which are the subject of sale to the investor.

Is it conceivable that the great house of Morgan would have aided in providing the New Haven with the hundreds of millions so unwisely expended, if its judgment had not been clouded by participation in the New Haven's management?

Chapter X

The Inefficiency of the Oligarchs

We must break the Money Trust or the Money Trust will break us. The Interstate Commerce Commission said in its report on the most disastrous of the recent wrecks on the New Haven Railroad:

> On this directorate were and are men whom the confiding public recognize as magicians in the art of finance, and wizards in the construction, operation, and consolidation of great systems of railroads. The public therefore rested secure that with the knowledge of the railroad art possessed by such men investments and travel should both be safe. Experience has shown that this reliance of the public was not justified as to either finance or safety.

This failure of banker-management is not surprising. The surprise is that men should have supposed it would succeed. For banker-management contravenes the fundamental laws of human limitations: *First,* that no man can serve two masters; *second,* that a man cannot at the same time do many things well.

Seeming Successes

There are numerous seeming exceptions to these rules; and a relatively few real ones. Of course, many banker-managed properties have been prosperous; some for a long time, at the expense of the public; some for a shorter time, because of the impetus attained before they were banker-managed. It is not difficult to have a large net income, where one has the field to oneself, has all the advantages privilege can give, and may "charge all the traffic will bear." And even in competitive business the success of a long-established, well-organized business with a widely extended goodwill, must continue for a considerable time; especially if buttressed by intertwined relations constantly giving it the preference over competitors. The real test of efficiency comes when success has to be struggled for; when natural or legal conditions limit the charges which may be made for the goods sold or service rendered. Our banker-managed railroads have recently been subjected to such a test, and they have failed to pass it. "It is only," says Goethe, "when working within limitations, that the master is disclosed."

Why Oligarchy Fails

Banker-management fails, partly because the private interest destroys soundness of judgment and undermines loyalty. It fails partly, also, because banker directors are led by their occupation (and often even by the mere fact of their location remote from the operated properties) to apply a false test in making their decisions. Prominent in the banker-direct mind is always this thought: "What will be the probable effect of our action upon the market value of the company's stock and bonds, or, indeed, generally upon stock exchange values?" The stock market is so much a part of the investment-banker's life, that he cannot help being affected by this consideration, however disinterested he may be. The stock market is sensitive. Facts are often misinterpreted "by the street" or by investors. And with the best of intentions, directors susceptible to such influences are led to unwise decisions in the effort to prevent misinterpretations. Thus, expenditures necessary for maintenance, or for the ultimate good of a property are often deferred by banker-directors, because of the belief that the making of them *now,* would (by showing smaller net earnings), create a bad, and even false, impression on the market. Dividends are paid which should not be, because of the effect which it is believed reduction or suspension would have upon the market value of the company's securities. To exercise a sound judgment in the difficult affairs of business is, at best, a delicate operation. And no man can successfully perform that function whose mind is diverted, however innocently, from the study of, "what is best in the long run for the company of which I am director?" The banker-director is peculiarly liable to such distortion of judgment by reason of his occupation and his environment. But there is a further reason why, ordinarily, banker-management must fail.

The Element of Time

The banker, with his multiplicity of interests, cannot ordinarily give the time essential to proper supervision and to acquiring that knowledge of the facts necessary to the exercise of sound judgment. The *Century Dictionary* tells us that a Director is "one who directs; one who guides, superintends, governs, and manages." Real efficiency in any business in which conditions are ever changing must ultimately depend, in large measure, upon the correctness of the judgment exercised, almost from day to day, on the important problems as they arise. And how can the leading bankers, necessarily engrossed in the problems of their own vast private businesses, get time to know and to correlate the facts concerning so many other complex businesses? Besides, they start usually with ignorance of the particular business which they are supposed to direct. When the last paper was signed which created the Steel Trust, one of the lawyers (as Mr. Perkins frankly tells us) said: "That signature is the last one necessary to put the Steel industry, on a large scale, into the hands of men who do not know anything about it."

Avocations of the Oligarchs

The New Haven System is not a railroad, but an agglomeration of a railroad plus 121 separate corporations, control of which was acquired by the New Haven after that railroad attained its full growth of about 2000 miles of line. In administering the railroad and each of the properties formerly managed through these 122 separate companies, there must arise from time to time difficult questions on which the directors should pass judgment. The real managing directors of the New Haven system during the decade of its decline were: J. Pierpont Morgan, George F. Baker, and William Rockefeller. Mr. Morgan was, until his death in 1913, the head of perhaps the largest banking house in the world. Mr. Baker was, until 1909, President and then Chairman of the Board of Directors of one of America's leading banks (the First National of New York), and Mr. Rockefeller was, until 1911, President of the Standard Oil Company. Each was well advanced in years. Yet each of these men, besides the duties of his own vast business, and important private interests, undertook to "guide, superintend, govern and manage," not only the New Haven but also the following other corporations, some of which were similarly complex: Mr. Morgan, 48 corporations, including 40 railroad corporations, with at least 100 subsidiary companies, and 16,000 miles of line; 3 banks and trust or insurance companies; 5 industrial and public-service companies. Mr. Baker, 48 corporations, including 15 railroad corporations, with at least 158 subsidiaries, and 37,400 miles of track; 18 banks, and trust or insurance companies; 15 public-service corporations and industrial concerns. Mr. Rockefeller, 37 corporations, including 23 railroad corporations with at least 117 subsidiary companies, and 26,400 miles of line; 5 banks, trust or insurance companies; 9 public service companies and industrial concerns.

Substitutes

It has been urged that in view of the heavy burdens which the leaders of finance assume in directing Business-America, we should be patient of error and refrain from criticism, lest the leaders be deterred from continuing to perform this public service. A very respectable Boston daily said a few days after Commissioner McChord's report on the North Haven wreck:

> It is believed that the New Haven pillory repeated with some frequency will make the part of railroad director quite undesirable and hard to fill, and more and more avoided by responsible men. Indeed it may even become so that men will have to be paid a substantial salary to compensate them in some degree for the risk involved in being on the board of directors.

But there is no occasion for alarm. The American people have as little need of oligarchy in business as in politics. There are thousands of men in America who could have performed for the New Haven stockholders the task of one "who guides, superintends, governs, and manages," better than did Mr. Morgan, Mr. Baker, and Mr. Rockefeller. For though possessing less native ability, even the average business man would have done better than they, because working under proper conditions. There is great strength in serving with singleness of purpose one master only. There is great strength in having time to give to a business the attention which its difficult problems demand. And tens of thousands more Americans could be rendered competent to guide our important businesses. Liberty is the greatest developer. Herodotus tells us that while the tyrants ruled, the Athenians were no better fighters than their neighbors; but when freed, they immediately surpassed all others. If industrial democracy—true cooperation—should be substituted for industrial absolutism, there would be no lack of industrial leaders.

England's Big Business

England, too, has big business. But her big business is the Cooperative Wholesale Society, with a wonderful story of 50 years of beneficent growth. Its annual turnover is now about $150,000,000—an amount exceeded by the sales of only a few American industrials; an amount larger than the gross receipts of any American railroad, except the Pennsylvania and the New York Central systems. Its business is very diversified, for its purpose is to supply the needs of its members. It includes that of wholesale dealer, of manufacturer, of grower, of miner, of banker, of insurer, and of carrier. It operates the biggest flour mills and the biggest shoe factory in all Great Britain. It manufactures woolen cloths, all kinds of men's, women's, and children's clothing, a dozen kinds of prepared foods, and as many household articles. It operates creameries. It carries on every branch of the printing business. It is now buying coal lands. It has a bacon factory in Denmark, and a tallow and oil factory in Australia. It grows tea in Ceylon. And through all the purchasing done by the Society runs this general principle: Go direct to the source of production, whether at home or abroad, so as to save commissions of middlemen and agents. Accordingly, it has buyers and warehouses in the United States, Canada, Australia, Spain, Denmark, and Sweden. It owns steamers plying between Continental and English ports. It has an important banking department; it insures the property and person of its members. Every one of these departments is conducted in competition with the most efficient concerns in their respective lines in Great Britain. The Cooperative Wholesale Society makes its purchases, and manufactures its products, in order to supply the 1399 local distributive, cooperative societies scattered over all England; but each local society is at liberty to buy from the wholesale society, or not, as it chooses; and they buy only if the Cooperative Wholesale sells at market prices. This the Cooperative actually does; and it is able besides to return to the local a fair dividend on its purchases.

Industrial Democracy

Now, how are the directors of this great business chosen? Not by England's leading bankers, or other notabilities, supposed to possess unusual wisdom; but democratically, by all of the people interested in the operations of the Society. And the number of such persons who have directly or indirectly a voice in the selection of the directors of the English Cooperative Wholesale Society is 2,750,000. For the directors of the Wholesale Society are elected by vote of the delegates of the 1399 retail societies. And the delegates of the retail societies are, in turn, selected by the members of the local societies—that is, by the consumers, on the principle of one man, one vote, regardless of the amount of capital contributed. Note what kind of men these industrial democrats select to exercise executive control of their vast organization. Not all-wise bankers or their dummies, but men who have risen from the ranks of cooperation; men who, by conspicuous service in the local societies have won the respect and confidence of their fellows. The directors are elected for one year only; but a director is rarely unseated. J. T. W. Mitchell was president of the Society continuously for 21 years. Thirty-two directors are selected in this manner. Each gives to the business of the Society his whole time and attention; and the aggregate salaries of the thirty-two is less than that of many a single executive in American corporations; for these directors of England's big business serve each for a salary of about $1500 a year.

The Cooperative Wholesale Society of England is the oldest and largest of these institutions. But similar wholesale societies exist in 15 other countries. The Scotch Society (which William Maxwell has served most efficiently as President for thirty years at a salary never exceeding $38 a week) has a turn-over of more than $50,000,000 a year.

A Remedy for Trusts

Albert Sonnichsen, General Secretary of the Cooperative League, tells in the *American Review of Reviews* for April, 1913, how the Swedish Wholesale Society curbed the Sugar Trust; how it crushed the Margarine Combine (compelling it to dissolve after having lost 2,300,000 crowns in the struggle); and how in Switzerland the Wholesale Society forced the dissolution of the Shoe Manufacturers Association. He tells also this memorable incident:

> Six years ago, at an international congress in Cremona, Dr. Hans Müller, a Swiss delegate, presented a resolution by which an international wholesale society should be created. Luigi Luzzatti, Italian Minister of State and an ardent member of the movement, was in the chair. Those who were present say Luzzatti paused, his eyes lighted up, then, dramatically raising his hand, he said: "Dr. Müller proposes to the assembly a great idea—that of opposing to the great trusts, the Rockefellers of the world, a world-wide cooperative alliance which shall become so powerful as to crush the trusts."

Cooperation in America

America has no Wholesale Cooperative Society able to grapple with the trusts. But it has some very strong retail societies, like the Tamarack of Michigan, which has distributed in dividends to its members $1,144,000 in 23 years. The recent high cost of living has greatly stimulated interest in the cooperative movement; and John Graham Brooks* reports that we have already about 350 local distributive societies. The movement toward federation is progressing. There are over 100 cooperative stores in Minnesota, Wisconsin, and other Northwestern states, many of which were organized by or through the zealous work of Mr. Tousley and his associates of the Right Relationship League and are in some ways affiliated. In New York City 83 organizations are affiliated with the Cooperative League. In New Jersey the societies have federated into the American

---

John Graham Brooks, a leading labor sociologist and reformer, was the first president of the National Consumers' League.

Cooperative Alliance of Northern New Jersey. In California, long the seat of effective cooperative work, a central management committee is developing. And progressive Wisconsin has recently legislated wisely to develop cooperation throughout the state. Among our farmers the interest in cooperation is especially keen. The federal government has just established a separate bureau of the Department of Agriculture to aid in the study, development, and introduction of the best methods of cooperation in the working of farms, in buying, and in distribution; and special attention is now being given to farm credits—a field of cooperation in which Continental Europe has achieved complete success, and to which David Lubin, America's delegate to the International Institute of Agriculture at Rome, has, among others, done much to direct our attention.

People's Savings Banks

The German farmer has achieved democratic banking. The 13,000 little cooperative credit associations, with an average membership of about 90 persons, are truly banks of the people, by the people, and for the people.

First: The banks' resources are *of* the people. These aggregate about $500,000,000. Of this amount $375,000,000 represents the farmers' savings deposits; $50,000,000, the farmers' current deposits; $6,000,000, the farmers' share capital; and $13,000,000, amounts earned and placed in the reserve. Thus, nearly nine-tenths of these large resources belong to the farmers—that is, to the members of the banks.

Second: The banks are managed *by* the people—that is, the members. And membership is easily attained; for the average amount of paid-up share capital was, in 1909, less than $5 per member. Each member has one vote regardless of the number of his shares or the amount of his deposits. These members elect the officers. The committees and trustees (and often even, the treasurer) serve without pay: so that the expenses of the banks are, on the average, about $150 a year.

Third: The banks are *for* the people. The farmers' money is loaned by the farmer to the farmer at a low rate of interest (usually 4 per cent. to 6 per cent.); the shareholders receiving, on their shares, the same rate of interest that the borrowers pay on their loans. Thus the resources of all farmers are made available to each farmer, for productive purposes.

This democratic rural banking is not confined to Germany. As Henry W. Wolff says in his book on cooperative banks:

> Propagating themselves by their own merits, little people's cooperative banks have overspread Germany, Italy, Austria, Hungary, Switzer-

land, Belgium. Russia is following up those countries; France is striving strenuously for the possession of cooperative credit. Servia [Serbia], Romania, and Bulgaria have made such credit their own. Canada has scored its first success on the road to its acquisition. Cyprus, and even Jamaica, have made their first start. Ireland has substantial first-fruits to show of her economic sowings. South Africa is groping its way to the same goal. Egypt has discovered the necessity of cooperative banks, even by the side of Lord Cromer's pet creation, the richly endowed "agricultural bank." India has made a beginning full of promise. And even in far Japan, and in China, people are trying to acclimatize the more perfected organizations of Schulze-Delitzsch and Raffeisen. The entire world seems girdled with a ring of cooperative credit. Only the United States and Great Britain still lag lamentably behind.

Bankers' Savings Banks

The saving banks of America present a striking contrast to these democratic banks. Our savings banks also have performed a great service. They have provided for the people's funds safe depositories with some income return. Thereby they have encouraged thrift and have created, among other things, reserves for the proverbial "rainy day." They have also discouraged "old stocking" hoarding, which diverts the money of the country from the channels of trade. American savings banks are also, in a sense, banks *of* the people; for it is the people's money which is administered by them. The $4,500,000,000 deposits in 2,000 American savings banks belong to about ten million people, who have an average deposit of about $450. But our savings banks are not banks *by* the people, nor, in the full sense, *for* the people.

First: American savings banks are not managed *by* the people. The stock-savings banks, most prevalent in the Middle West and the South, are purely commercial enterprises, managed, of course, by the stockholders' representatives. The mutual savings banks, most prevalent in the Eastern states, have no stockholders; but the depositors have no voice in the management. The banks are managed by trustees *for* the people, practically a self-constituted and self-perpetuating body, composed of "leading" and, to a large extent, public-spirited citizens. Among them (at least in the larger cities) there is apt to be a predominance of investment bankers, and bank directors. Thus the three largest savings banks of Boston (whose aggregate deposits exceed those of the other 18 banks) have together 81 trustees. Of these, 52 are investment bankers or directors in other Massachusetts banks or trust companies.

Second: The funds of our savings banks (whether stock or purely mutual) are not used mainly *for* the people. The depositors are allowed interest (usually from 3 to 4 per cent.). In the mutual savings banks they receive ultimately all the net earnings. But the money gathered in these reservoirs is not used to aid *productively* persons of the classes who make the deposits. The depositors are largely wage earners, salaried people, or members of small tradesmen's families. Statically the money is used for them. Dynamically it is used for the capitalist. For rare, indeed, are the instances when savings banks moneys are loaned to advance productively one of the depositor class. Such persons would seldom be able to provide the required security; and it is doubtful whether their small needs would, in any event, receive consideration. In 1912 the largest of Boston's mutual savings banks—the Provident Institution for Savings, which is the pioneer mutual savings bank of America—managed $53,000,000 of people's money. Nearly one-half of the resources ($24,262,072) was invested in bonds—state, municipal, railroad, railway, and telephone—and in bank stock; or was deposited in national banks or trust companies. Two-fifths of the resources ($20,764,770) were loaned on real estate mortgages; and the average amount of a loan was $52,569. One-seventh of the resources ($7,566,612) was loaned on personal security; and the average of each of these loans was $54,830. Obviously, the "small man" is not conspicuous among the borrowers; and these large-scale investments do not even serve the individual depositor especially well; for this bank pays its depositors a rate of interest lower than the average. Even our admirable Postal Savings Bank system serves productively mainly the capitalist. These postal saving stations are in effect catch-basins merely, which collect the people's money for distribution among the national banks.

Progress

Alphonse Desjardins of Levis, Province of Quebec, has demonstrated that cooperative credit associations are applicable, also, to at least some urban communities. Levis, situated on the St. Lawrence opposite the City of Quebec, is a city of 8,000 inhabitants. Desjardins himself is a man of the people. Many years ago he became impressed with the fact that the people's savings were not utilized primarily to aid the people productively. There were then located in Levis branches of three ordinary banks of deposit—a mutual savings bank, the postal savings bank, and three incorporated "loaners"; but the people were not served. After much thinking, he chanced to read of the European rural banks. He proceeded to work out the idea for use in Levis; and in 1900 established there the first "credit-union." For seven years he watched carefully the operations of this little bank. The pioneer union had accumulated in that period $80,000 in resources. It had made 2900 loans to its members, aggregating $350,000; the loans averaging $120 in amount, and the interest rate 6½ per cent. In all this time the bank had *not met with a single loss*. Then Desjardins concluded that democratic banking was applicable to Canada; and he proceeded to establish other credit-unions. In the last 5 years the number of credit-unions in the Province of Quebec has grown to 121; and 19 have been established in the Province of Ontario. Desjardins was not merely the pioneer. All the later credit-unions also have been established through his aid; and 24 applications are now in hand requesting like assistance from him. Year after year that aid has been given without pay by this public-spirited man of large family and small means, who lives as simply as the ordinary mechanic. And it is noteworthy that this rapidly extending system of cooperative credit-banks has been established in Canada wholly without government aid, Desjardins having given his services free, and his traveling expenses having been paid by those seeking his assistance.

In 1909, Massachusetts, under Desjardin's guidance, enacted a law for the incorporation of credit-unions. The first union established in Springfield, in 1910, was named after Herbert Myrick—a strong advocate of cooperative finance. Since then 25 other unions have been formed; and the names of the unions and of their officers disclose that 11 are Jewish, 8 French-Canadian, and 2 Italian—a strong indication that the immigrant is not unprepared for financial democracy. There is reason to believe that these people's banks will spread rapidly in the United States and that they will succeed. For the cooperative building and loan associations, managed by wage-earners and salary-earners, who joined together for systematic saving and ownership of houses—have prospered in many states. In Massachusetts, where they have existed for 35 years, their success has been notable—the number, in 1912, being 162, and their aggregate assets nearly $75,000,000.

Thus farmers, workingmen, and clerks are learning to use their little capital and their savings to help one another instead of turning over their money to the great bankers for safe keeping, and to be themselves exploited. And may we not expect that when the cooperative movement develops in America, merchants and manufacturers will learn from farmers and working-men how to help themselves by helping one another, and thus join in attaining the New Freedom for all? When merchants and manufacturers learn this lesson, money kings will lose subjects, and swollen fortunes may shrink; but industries will flourish, because the faculties of men will be liberated and developed.

President Wilson has said wisely:

> No country can afford to have its prosperity originated by a small controlling class. The treasury of America does not lie in the brains of the small body of men now in control of the great enterprises. . . . It depends upon the inventions of unknown men, upon the originations of unknown men, upon the ambitions of unknown men. Every country is renewed out of the ranks of the unknown, not out of the ranks of the already famous and powerful in control.

A Brandeis Chronology
(1856–1941)

1856

November 13: Louis D. Brandeis born in Louisville, Kentucky.

1859

Edwin L. Drake strikes first oil well in Pennsylvania.

1866

Cyrus Field lays transatlantic telegraph cable.

1868

Christopher Sholes invents typewriter.

1870

John D. Rockefeller founds Standard Oil.

1873

Andrew Carnegie opens steel works in Pittsburgh.

1875

September: Brandeis enrolls in the Harvard Law School.

1876

March 7: Alexander Graham Bell receives patent for telephone.

1877

June: Brandeis graduates first in his class from law school.
July: Federal troops called out in great railroad strike.
September: Brandeis begins one year of graduate study.

1878

September: Brandeis begins law practice in St. Louis.

1879

July: Brandeis returns to Boston and establishes law partnership with Samuel Warren.

1881

December: American Federation of Labor founded.

1882

Rockefeller creates the Standard Oil trust, the first trust in the U.S., to control his oil holdings.

1883

Pendleton Act creates civil service in federal government.

1884

First skyscraper built in Chicago.

1886

May 1: Police attack socialist demonstration in Haymarket riot.

October 28: Statute of Liberty dedicated in New York Harbor.

1887

Interstate Commerce Act passed.

1889

Jane Addams opens Hull House in Chicago.

Brandeis dissolves partnership with Warren.

November: Brandeis argues first case before U.S. Supreme Court.

1890

July 2: Sherman Antitrust Act passed.

October 4: Brandeis becomes engaged to Alice Goldmark.

December: With Warren, Brandeis publishes article "Right to Privacy."

1891

March 23: Brandeis marries Alice Goldmark.

1892

July: Homestead strike pits steel workers against armed guards in violent struggle.

1893

February 27:   First daughter, Susan, born to Brandeises.

1895

January 21:   Supreme Court, in *U.S. v. E. C. Knight,* weakens Sherman Antitrust Act.

1896

April 25:   Second daughter, Elizabeth, born.

May 18:   Supreme Court in *Plessy v. Ferguson* permits racial segregation.

1897

January 11:   Brandeis testifies against Dingley Tariff before House Ways and Means Committee (first appearance before congressional committee).

April 30:   Brandeis becomes involved in fight against charter revision of Boston Elevated Railroad.

Boston opens first subway in America.

1898

April 25:   Congress declares war on Spain.

1900

November: Robert M. La Follette elected governor of Wisconsin.

1901

February: U.S. Steel Corporation organized at $1 billion capitalization.

September 6:   President McKinley assassinated.

September 14:   Theodore Roosevelt becomes president.

1902

January: Brandeis drafts bill to reduce political activity of public service corporations.

1903

December 17:   Wright Brothers make first powered flight at Kitty Hawk, N.C.

1904

March 14: *Northern Securities* case revivifies Sherman Act.

March: Ida Tarbell publishes exposé of Standard Oil trust.

May 2: Public Franchise League begins its fight for fair valuation of consolidated gas company stock.

1905

March 13: Brandeis proposes sliding scale rates for gas company.

April 18: Brandeis retained as counsel by policyholders in investigation of the great insurance company scandals.

May 4: Brandeis delivers speech, "The Opportunity in the Law," to Harvard Ethical Society.

October 26: Brandeis first proposes idea of savings bank life insurance.

1906

Upton Sinclair publishes *The Jungle*.

Meat Inspection Act passed.

Henry Ford produces his first automobile.

May 26: Sliding scale rate schedule enacted into law.

September 15: Brandeis publishes "Wage-Earner's Life Insurance" in *Collier's*.

November 26: Massachusetts Savings Bank Insurance League organized.

1907

June 26: Savings bank insurance enacted into law.

June 29: Brandeis begins fight against Morgan-sponsored merger of the New Haven and the Boston and Maine Railroads.

1908

January 15: Brandeis argues *Muller v. Oregon* before U.S. Supreme Court.

February 24: *Muller* case decided in support of Oregon maximum hours law.

June 18: First savings bank in Massachusetts opens insurance department.

1909

March 4: William Howard Taft sworn in as president.

September 13: Taft exonerates Ballinger from Pinchot-Glavis charges.

November 11: *Collier's Weekly* publishes Glavis report.

1910

January 7:   Brandeis retained as counsel in Ballinger case.

January 26:   Joint congressional committee begins hearings on Ballinger charges.

May 14:   Evidence submitted showing that Taft predated exoneration letter.

July 21:   Brandeis enters New York garment workers' strike as mediator.

August: Brandeis agrees to represent shippers in rate hearings before Interstate Commerce Commission.

August 31:   Theodore Roosevelt delivers "New Nationalism" speech in Ossowatomie, Kansas.

November: Woodrow Wilson elected governor of New Jersey.

November 1:   Brandeis claims railroads could save a million dollars a day by using scientific management.

December: National Progressive Republican League formed to advance Robert M. La Follette as 1912 Republican presidential candidate.

1911

Triangle fire kills 146 garment workers.

January 17:   Brandeis makes argument before Interstate Commerce Commission in Advanced Freight case.

February 13:   ICC rejects rate increase.

March 7:   Richard Ballinger resigns as secretary of the interior.

November 28:   Brandeis publishes article, "Using Other People's Money," in *New York American*.

December 14:   Brandeis gives antitrust testimony before Senate Committee on Interstate Commerce.

1912

January 26–27:   Brandeis testifies on antitrust matters before House Judiciary Committee.

January 29–30:   Brandeis testifies before Stanley Committee on U.S. Steel.

July 2:   Democrats nominate Woodrow Wilson for president.

July 10:   Brandeis publicly endorses Wilson.

Roosevelt bolts Republican Party and becomes independent candidate for president.

August 13:   Brandeis meets Jacob de Haas, who introduces him to Zionism.

August 28: Brandeis and Wilson meet for first time in Sea Girt, New Jersey.

October 15: Norman Hapgood fired as editor of *Collier's Weekly.*

November 5: Wilson elected president.

1913

February 25: Sixteenth Amendment permits income taxes.

March 4: Wilson sworn in as president.

March 10: Brandeis makes first trip to Washington to consult with administration.

May 31: Seventeenth Amendment provides for direct election of senators.

June Norman Hapgood assumes editorial control of *Harper's Weekly.*

June 11: Brandeis meets with Wilson to determine final shape of banking bill.

August 16: "Banker-Management: Why It Has Failed" published in *Harper's Weekly.*

October 3: Underwood-Simmons Tariff becomes law.

November 22: Brandeis publishes "Breaking the Money Trust"

December 23: Federal Reserve system enacted into law.

1914

Henry Ford introduces assembly line in his factories.

January 3: J. P. Morgan Company resigns from thirty directorships.

January 20: Wilson delivers antitrust message.

March: *Other People's Money* published in book form.

August 1: War breaks out in Europe.

August 30: Brandeis accepts chairmanship of emergency Zionist committee.

September 26: Federal Trade Commission Act becomes law.

October 15: Clayton Antitrust Act signed into law.

1916

January 28: Wilson nominates Brandeis to the U.S. Supreme Court.

May 24: Judiciary Committee approves Brandeis nomination.

June 1: Full Senate confirms nomination, 47–22.

June 5: Brandeis sworn in as associate justice of the Supreme Court.

July 21: Brandeis resigns official positions in Zionist groups.

November 7:   Wilson reelected to a second term.

1917

January 22:   Wilson delivers "Peace without Victory" speech.

April 6:   United States declares war on Central Powers.

November 2:   Great Britain issues Balfour Declaration.

1918

January 8:   Wilson proposes "Fourteen Points."

November 11:   Armistice ends World War I.

December: First American Jewish Congress meets in Philadelphia.

1919

January 18:   Versailles Peace Conference opens.

January 29:   Eighteenth Amendment prohibits the manufacture and sale of alcoholic beverages.

July 8:   Brandeis arrives in Palestine on fact-finding tour.

October 28:   Congress passes Volstead Act, reinforcing the Eighteenth Amendment, over Wilson's veto.

1920

April 20:   Palestine awarded to Great Britain as a mandate.

August 26:   Nineteenth Amendment gives women the vote.

November 2:   Warren Harding elected president.

1939

February 13:   Brandeis resigns from Supreme Court.

1941

October 5:   Brandeis dies in Washington, D.C.

Questions for Consideration

1. What is the main theme of *Other People's Money?*
2. Brandeis suggested the title for a specific purpose. What do you think that purpose is?
3. Brandeis was a great believer in facts. How does he use facts to make his case? Do you find this use persuasive?
4. Brandeis, like other muckrakers, used a variety of techniques to make his points. What are some of the literary techniques he uses in this work?
5. As a historical document, what does *Other People's Money* tell us about the Progressive era?
6. Does Brandeis castigate all bankers? Which bankers, if any, merit his approval?
7. What does Brandeis see as a banker's main functions? What role, if any, does Brandeis claim the bankers played in initiating big businesses such as railroads, steel, and telephone? What is the relation, as Brandeis sees it, between initiation and combination?
8. Given the argument Brandeis makes, why do you think some Progressives nonetheless welcomed big business?
9. Although Brandeis is constantly attacking bigness, is he most opposed to bigness itself or to the abuses he claims must accompany bigness?
10. Brandeis spends a lot of time talking about railroads. Why were railroads so important to his indictment of the banks?
11. What is Brandeis's opinion of "interlocking directorates"? What effect does he claim they have on society?
12. *Other People's Money* is not about only banking and finance. What social, moral, and political effects does Brandeis claim banking and finance have on society?
13. What does Brandeis propose as the only way to break the money trust?
14. If bigness is bad, as Brandeis suggests, what alternative vision does he hold out as an ideal for America?
15. Do you agree with Brandeis that a person can "serve one master only"? Why or why not?
16. Modern economists do not agree with Brandeis's claim that big business is inefficient. In what areas would you think that big businesses are more efficient than small, and what are the social consequences of this efficiency?

17. If you were writing a revised edition of *Other People's Money* today, what examples would you use to show that Brandeis's arguments about monopoly are still valid?

18. If you were asked to write a rebuttal to this work, what examples could you use to show that banks and big business are not harmful to a democratic society?

19. What part of Brandeis's argument about the problems posed by big industry remain valid in the 1990s?

20. What are some contemporary events or situations that parallel the abuses by big bankers that Brandeis details?

Selected Bibliography

COLLECTIONS OF BRANDEIS'S WRITINGS

Brandeis, Louis D. *Business: A Profession.* Boston: Small, Maynard, 1914.

Fraenkel, Osmond K., ed. *The Curse of Bigness.* New York: Viking, 1934.

Goldman, Solomon, ed. *Brandeis on Zionism.* Washington, D.C.: Zionist Organization of America, 1942.

———. *The Words of Justice Brandeis.* New York: Henry Schuman, 1953.

Lief, Alfred, ed. *The Brandeis Guide to the Modern World.* Boston: Little, Brown, 1941.

———. *The Social and Economic Views of Mr. Justice Brandeis.* New York: Vanguard Press, 1930.

Strum, Philippa, ed. *Brandeis on Democracy.* Lawrence: University Press of Kansas, 1994.

Urofsky, Melvin I., and David W. Levy, eds. *Letters of Louis D. Brandeis.* 5 vols. Albany: State University of New York Press, 1971–1978.

BIOGRAPHIES

Gal, Alon. *Brandeis of Boston.* Cambridge: Harvard University Press, 1980.

Mason, Alpheus T. *Brandeis: A Free Man's Life.* New York: Viking, 1946.

Paper, Louis J. *Brandeis.* Englewood Cliffs: Prentice-Hall, 1983.

Strum, Philippa. *Brandeis: Justice for the People.* Cambridge: Harvard University Press, 1984.

Urofsky, Melvin I. *Louis D. Brandeis and the Progressive Tradition.* Boston: Little, Brown, 1981.

WORKS ON VARIOUS ASPECTS OF BRANDEIS'S CAREER

Abrams, Richard M. *Conservatism in a Progressive Era: Massachusetts Politics, 1900–1912.* Cambridge: Harvard University Press, 1964.

Baskerville, Stephen W. *Of Laws and Limitations: An Intellectual Portrait of Louis Dembitz Brandeis.* Rutherford: Fairleigh Dickinson University Press, 1994.

Bickel, Alexander M., ed. *The Unpublished Opinions of Mr. Justice Brandeis.* Cambridge: Harvard University Press, 1957.

Burt, Robert A. *Two Jewish Justices: Outcasts in the Promised Land.* Berkeley: University of California Press, 1988.

Dawson, Nelson, ed. *Brandeis and America.* Lexington: University Press of Kentucky, 1989.

Frankfurter, Felix, ed. *Mr. Justice Brandeis.* New Haven: Yale University Press, 1932.

Halpern, Ben. *A Clash of Heroes: Brandeis, Weismann, and American Zionism.* New York: Oxford University Press, 1987.

Konefsky, Samuel J. *The Legacy of Holmes and Brandeis.* New York: Macmillan, 1956.

McCraw, Thomas K. *Prophets of Regulation.* Cambridge: Harvard University Press, 1984.

Mason, Alpheus T. *The Brandeis Way: A Case Study in the Workings of Democracy.* Princeton: Princeton University Press, 1938.

Strum, Philippa. *Brandeis: Beyond Progressivism.* Lawrence: University Press of Kansas, 1993.

Urofsky, Melvin I. *American Zionism from Herzl to the Holocaust.* Garden City, N.Y.: Anchor Press/Doubleday, 1975.

WORKS ON THEODORE ROOSEVELT
AND WOODROW WILSON

Blum, John Morton. *The Republican Roosevelt.* Cambridge: Harvard University Press, 1954.

———. *Woodrow Wilson and the Politics of Morality.* Boston: Little, Brown, 1956.

Cooper, John Milton, Jr. *The Warrior and the Priest: Woodrow Wilson and Theodore Roosevelt.* Cambridge: Harvard University Press, 1983.

Harbough, William. *Power and Responsibility: The Life and Times of Theodore Roosevelt.* New York: Octagon Books, 1975.

Link, Arthur S. *Woodrow Wilson.* 5 vols. Princeton: Princeton University Press, 1947–1965.

WORKS ON THE PROGRESSIVE ERA

Hays, Samuel P. *The Response to Industrialism, 1885–1914.* Chicago: University of Chicago Press, 1957.

Link, Arthur S. *Woodrow Wilson and the Progressive Era, 1910–1917.* New York: Harper and Row, 1954.

Mowry, George E. *The Era of Theodore Roosevelt, 1901–1910.* New York: Harper and Row, 1958.

West, Robert Craig. *Banking Reform and the Federal Reserve, 1863–1923.* Ithaca: Cornell University Press, 1977.

Wiebe, Robert. *The Search for Order, 1877–1920.* New York: Hill and Wang, 1967.

Index